China's Agriculture and Rural Development in the Post-Reform Era

By Feng Jun, Wang Youming,
Hu Yunchao and Yu Ji

Published by
ACA Publishing Ltd.
University House
11-13 Lower Grosvenor Place,
London SW1W 0EX, UK
Tel: +44 (0)20 7834 7676 Fax: +44 (0)20 7973 0076
E-mail: info@alaincharlesasia.com

Web: www.alaincharlesasia.com
Beijing Office
Tel:+86(0)10 8472 1250 Fax:86(0)10 5885 0639
Written by Feng Jun, Wang Youming, Hu Yunchao, Yu Ji
Edited by Martin Savery, ACA Publishing Ltd
Translated by Huang Xiean
© People's Publishing House, 2015
This translation is published by ACA Publishing Ltd in association with People's Publishing House

ALL RIGHTS RESERVED. NO PART OF THIS
PUBLICATION MAY BE REPRODUCED IN MATERIAL FORM,
BY ANY MEANS, WHETHER GRAPHIC,
ELECTRONIC, MECHANICAL OR OTHER, INCLUDING
PHOTOCOPYING OR INFORMATION STORAGE, IN
WHOLE OR IN PART, AND MAY NOT BE USED TO PREPARE
OTHER PUBLICATIONS WITHOUT WRITTEN
PERMISSION FROM THE PUBLISHER.

The greatest care has been taken to ensure accuracy but the publisher can accept no responsibility for errors or omissions, or for any liability occasioned by relying on its content.
ISBN 978-1-910760-11-6
China's Agriculture and Rural Development in the Post-Reform Era is available from the National Bibliographic Service of the British Library.

Preface

What is the state system of China? How has the Communist Party of China (CPC) managed to exercize long-term governance and to lead the Chinese people from one victory to another? What are the 'secrets' of the CPC's governance? What is China's development road? What significant strategies have been adopted in China? What is the next step in China's development? Why has China been able to achieve such rapid economic development? These are just some of the many questions frequently asked by the international community, especially foreign political parties and statesmen on their visits to China. For the purpose of providing answers to these questions and enabling readers to be informed about the real China and the CPC, we arranged for the *Understanding Modern China* Series (hereinafter referred to as the Series) to be written, to serve as elementary documents introducing the CPC, as well as China's development road, development theories and development experience.

The Series is inspired by the new philosophies, new ideas and new strategies for the country's governance put forward by General Secretary Xi Jinping since the 18th National Congress of the CPC, aimed at the following aspects: strenuously reflecting the development vision of 'the Chinese Dream' and the development prospects of the 'Two Centenary' goals; strenuously reflecting the coordinated promotion of the overall situation of a 'five-pronged approach to building socialism with Chinese characteristics to build up socialist economy, socialist democracy, socialist advanced culture, socialist harmonious society and socialist ecological civilisation; and the strategic arrangements for the 'Four-Pronged Comprehensive Strategy' comprehensively completing the building of a moderately prosperous society in all respects, comprehensively deepening reform in all respects, comprehensively advancing the rule of law, and comprehensively exercising strict discipline for the party; strenuously reflecting the 'new normal' facilitating and leading China's economic development and the implementation of the 'five major development concepts' to promote innovative, coordinated, green, open and shared development; strenuously reflecting the three major economic development strategies of the 'Belt and Road', the coordinated development of Beijing, Tianjin and Hebei province, and the Yangtze river economic belt. On the basis of a great number of fresh cases and experiences, the Series tells China's story, transmits China's voice, analyzes China's problems, and offers China solutions.

The Series has been written on the basis of telling China's story and transmitting China's voice, oriented around the following four aspects: the first is to illustrate the new measures taken to deepen reform since the 18th National Congress of the CPC, the new ideas on economic development and the new philosophy on foreign affairs, on the basis of an all-round introduction to the achievements since the reform and opening up; the second is to analyze the reason for the achievements, the underlying operating law, and the process of evolution, while presenting the development achievements of China's economy and society; the third is to keep to problem orientation and demand orientation, rather than attempt to be all-embracing and systematic, so as to clear up targeted doubts and confusion on the basis of the demands of foreign readers; the fourth is to introduce China not only in terms of 'where it is coming from', but also in terms of 'where it is going', for the purpose of enabling readers to know about China's historical development process on the one hand, and on the other hand, exemplifying and clarifying how China assures the organic unification of its past, present and future, the organic combination of legacy and innovation, and how China is planning its future development.

Under the guidance of the International Department of the CPC Central Committee, the writing of the Series has been organized by China Executive Leadership Academy Pudong (CELAP).

The International Department of the CPC Central Committee is the functional department of the CPC in charge of foreign affairs. So far, the CPC has established connections of various types with more than 600 political parties and organizations in over 160 countries and regions, which include left-wing and right-wing parties; both ruling parties and opposition parties. Foreign affairs work is of paramount importance to the CPC, and an indispensable component of national diplomacy as a whole, whose target is to promote state-to-state and people-to-people communication and understanding.

Preface

CELAP is a national leadership institution in China, and as a platform on which international cooperative training and exchange are carried out, CELAP has held fast to its characteristics of internationality and openness since March 2005 when it was founded. CELAP spares no effort in implementing international cooperative training, with target participants being foreign political parties and statesmen, high-ranking business executives and senior professionals. By the end of 2015, CELAP had offered training programs to more than 6,000 participants from over 130 countries, and thus has won wide recognition and received a favorable reception from the countries, regions and participants that are involved.

To cater for the needs of foreign participants, CELAP initiated the writing of the Series at the beginning of 2012, and after four years of modifications and improvements, the finalized manuscripts were completed at the end of 2015. The first batch of 10 books to be published in this Series are: *China's New Strategies for Governing the Country; The Communist Party of China: the Past, Present and Future of Party Building; China's Reform, Opening Up and Construction of Development Zones; The Framework of the Chinese Government and Public Services; A New Analysis of Urbanization in China; China's Agriculture and Rural Development in the Post-Reform Era; The Evolution of China's Diplomacy in the Modern Era; Leadership Selection and Appointment in China; Leadership Education and Training in China;* and *Shanghai – the 'Pacesetter' of China's Reform and Opening Up.*

The authors of the Series are mainly professionals in CELAP, and functionaries and specialists in the Development Research Center of the Shanghai Municipal People's Government, Shanghai Institute for International Studies and Hangzhou Research Center for Urban Studies.

The Series is published in Chinese and English, with the English translation done mainly by senior professors at Shanghai International Studies University, to whom thanks are due. Gratitude also goes to the People's Publishing House for its great support and positive suggestions in the process of writing and translating.

Writing such a series of textbooks for mature foreign students is a first in China. Constructive criticism is welcome, for the Series as a new endeavor can hardly be free from mistakes.

Editorial Committee of the *Understanding Modern China* Series
January 2016

The Editorial Committee of the Understanding Modern China Series

Directors: Guo Yezhou Feng Jun

Vice Directors: Zhou Zhongfei   An Yuejun

Members: (Listed alphabetically)

An Yuejun	Chen Zhong	Feng Jun
Guo Yezhou	He Lisheng	Jiang Haishan
Li Man	Li Yanhui	Liu Genfa
Liu Jingbei	Wang Guoping	Wang Jinding
Yang Jiemian	Zhao Shiming	Zheng Jinzhou
Zhou Zhenhua	Zhou Zhongfei	

Editor-in-Chief: Feng Jun

Alain Charles Asia (ACA) Publishing Ltd is delighted to be associated with the People's Publishing House to bring this series of 10 *Understanding Modern China* books to an English-speaking readership.

ACA, formerly known as ACP (Alain Charles Publishing) Ltd Beijing, was founded in October 1989 and was the first foreign-owned publishing company to be allowed to open an office in China.

In 2007, ACP Beijing was renamed ACA Publishing Ltd to better reflect its focus on China and the Asia-Pacific region. The company specialises in publishing books about China for international readers and has offices in Beijing and London.

ACA Publishing Ltd,

April 2016

Contents

Introduction X

    I. Objectives X
    II. Scope XI
    III. Key Points XIII
    IV. Reading Suggestions XIII

1. Main Systems of China's Agriculture, Rural Areas and Farmers 1

    I. The Current Situation of China's Agriculture, Rural Areas and Farmers 1
    II. The Course of Structural Reform in Rural Areas 3
    III. Rural Land System and Basic Operational System 7
    IV. Development of Township and Village Enterprises (TVEs).... 19
    V. The Governance Structure of Towns and Villages 23

2. How to Promote the Modernization of China's Agriculture ...28

    I. Safeguarding National Food Security 30
    II. Promote Strategic Restructuring of Agriculture 39
    III. Accelerate Agricultural Scientific and Technological Innovation and the Widespread Application of Technology 45
    IV. Improving Agricultural Facilities and Equipment 49
    V. Strengthening the Organization of Agricultural 51

3. How to Carry Out Construction of a New Countryside in China 60

    I. Strengthening the Construction of Rural Infrastructure 63
    II. Accelerating the Development of Social Undertakings in Rural Areas 69
    III. Raising the Rural Social Security Level 72
    IV. Improving Rural Environment Conservation and Rehabilitation 74
    V. Improving Rural Development System Mechanisms 77

4. How To Increase Chinese Farmers' Incomes and Make Them Rich 84
   I. Optimizing the Potential to Increase Rural Incomes 85
   II. Actively Develop Secondary and Tertiary Industries in Agriculture 90
   III. Developing Expansion of the County-Level Economy 97
   IV. Promoting the Employment of Rural Migrants 100
   V. Striving to Increase Transfer Income for Rural Workers 102

Introduction

I. Objectives

In the late 1970s, China kicked off a series of reforms in its rural areas. Since then, world-shaking changes have taken place and agriculture production has increased. China has ranked first in the world by output of grain, oil, vegetables, fruit, eggs and aquatic products for many consecutive years, creating a miracle of feeding nearly 20% of the world's population with 9% of its arable land. Rural economic development has been achieved through a balanced and all-round development of farming, forestry, animal husbandry and fishery. Based on quality production, optimal regional arrangements, industrialization and standardized management, modern agriculture has basically taken shape. The fast development of secondary and tertiary industries in rural areas has changed the employment structure and promoted development in small towns. The great improvements in farmers' living standards and their increased income have turned China from a country lacking basic necessities into a moderately affluent society, and China has become the first country to achieve the United Nations (UN) Millennium Development Goal of halving the number of its people living in poverty. Rural public services including education, healthcare and social security have greatly improved.

China's successful rural reforms have accumulated a rich store of experience for transforming its economic systems and attracted worldwide attention. China is willing to exchange ideas and share its best practices, address resource and environmental challenges together with other countries, and make life better for all, which is part of our globalization initiatives. According to *The State of World Food Insecurity 2012* released by the UN Food and Agriculture Organization (UNFAO), among the 868 million

Introduction

(868m) people who are chronically malnourished and even more who suffer from hunger, 850m are living in the rural areas of developing countries. It is of great importance for nations to communicate, share and make common efforts, and this book is published to make a contribution in this regard. It introduces the basic systems in rural China and elaborates how China promotes modern agriculture based on specific local conditions, builds a new countryside and helps farmers become rich despite having a large population and limited arable land and resources. Case studies are provided for better understanding.

We sincerely hope to give our readers, especially those who are foreign officials, experts and researchers who may come for communication and research to the China Executive Leadership Academy Pudong (CELAP), a sound understanding of China's agriculture and rural development through this book and also answers to the questions which they may be interested in such as how China safeguards food security, alleviates poverty and helps farmers get rich. It will be a great honor for us if the book inspires agriculture and rural development in other developing countries.

II. Scope

This book is divided into four chapters. Chapter One provides a brief introduction to China's agriculture, rural areas, farmers and rural systems, which will help readers gain an overall understanding about the development of China's agriculture and rural areas since the initiation of the reform and opening-up program and the current situation. The second, third and fourth chapters respectively focus on agricultural development, rural construction and farmers' income growth.

Chapter One introduces the basic conditions of China's agriculture, rural areas and farmers, the development of economic and organizational systems, including the household contract responsibility system, the rural land ownership system, the rural enterprise development system and the rural governance system. Section one of this Chapter gives a brief account of the basic conditions of China's agriculture, rural areas and farmers. Section two provides the background and an overview of the course of China's rural reform which mainly covers three important stages: 1) the combination of centralized and decentralized management on the basis of household contractual management in the late 1970s; 2) the agricultural products circulation system reform and the market-oriented reform of the rural economy starting in the

1980s; and 3) the coordination of urban and rural development since the early 21st century. Section three digs deeper into the rural land tenure system and the two-tier management system that combines centralized and decentralized management on the basis of household contractual management. Section four recounts how the expansion of township enterprises has promoted secondary and tertiary industries and forecasts their future development. Section five describes the rural governance structure which is composed of township-level local government administration and village-level self-governance.

Chapter Two focuses on how China promotes agricultural modernization. After a brief review of the progress made in China's agriculture, a detailed account is given in five dimensions. Section one introduces the measures adopted by the Chinese government to stabilize grain production. The stabilization of grain production is a perennially important strategy as it is critical for safeguarding food security. Section two describes the direction of the strategic structural adjustment of China's agriculture. The adjustment aims to enable the agricultural sector to create more economic benefits. Section three discusses how to promote technological innovation and applications in agriculture. Sections four and five are about agricultural modernization policies and measures: the improvement of agricultural facilities and equipment, and systemization and institutionalization of agricultural production and operation.

Chapter Three focuses on the construction of the new countryside since 2005. After an introduction to the background, it gives a detailed account of the progress and implementation measures. Section one is about improving rural infrastructure, including drinking water, power supply, clean energy, rural roads, housing, poverty relief, development and the follow-up support for migrants from reservoir construction sites. Section two talks about speeding up rural social services, including education, healthcare, culture, sports and employment services. Section three introduces the efforts made by the Chinese government to improve social security and address farmers' concerns by building a sound pension, healthcare and social assistance system under the principles of providing basic benefits, achieving full coverage, covering multiple levels, and ensuring flexibility and sustainability. Section four is about how the rural environment and living conditions are improved through developing circular agriculture and improving rural production. Section five discusses how to improve the rural economic system by promoting rural reform and institutional innovation.

Introduction

Chapter Four explores how to narrow the rural-urban income gap and increase farmers' incomes. Farmers' incomes mainly come from business operation, salary and fiscal transfers. Section one is about creating added value through agricultural industrialization, developing 'leisure agriculture' and tapping the grain production potential by helping villages specialize in a certain field based on local conditions. Section two is about increasing famers' incomes through the development of secondary and tertiary industries in rural areas, by promoting agricultural product processing, the growth of township enterprises, producer services and consumer services. Section three is about developing the county-level economy by transferring rural labor to non-agricultural industries and urban areas. Section four focuses on helping farmers find jobs in cities through providing vocational training and employment information, supporting farmers to start up their own businesses and protecting their labor rights. Section five is about increasing farmers' transfer income and introduces China's development support and poverty alleviation policies in terms of tax breaks, subsidies and social security.

III. Key Points

This book aims to introduce the institutional concepts and practical policies adopted by the Chinese government to promote China's agricultural and rural development over the past three decades, thereby giving foreign readers a basic understanding of how China's rural reform fits into China's overall reform and opening-up program. A knowledge of China's national conditions and political and economic systems is essential to develop a good understanding.

IV. Reading Suggestions

In order to gain a good understanding, we suggest: first, reading through Chapter One to understand China's agricultural and rural situation and the economic and social systems in the rural areas, which will help you understand the rural reform policies in the following chapters; second, trying to answer the questions at the end of each chapter which will help you find out more; and third, evaluating the references listed at the end of each chapter which will be a good tool for further study.

Since the book attempts to make a succinct and systematic analysis and summary of China's agriculture, rural areas and farmers, it is nearly impossible to detail everything. So if you have the opportunity to make field trips, you will get a better understanding of China's agricultural and rural development and the efforts made by Chinese farmers to pursue a happy life.

Chapter 1

Main Systems of China's Agriculture, Rural Areas and Farmers

I. The Current Situation of China's Agriculture, Rural Areas and Farmers

China is a large developing country with a population of 1.347bn in 2011, with nearly half living in rural areas. In some sense, China is sustaining a large population with relatively limited arable land. Improving agricultural production, ensuring food security and increasing famers' incomes have always been the primary goals of China's economic development. The Communist Party of China (CPC) and the State Council have made agriculture a top priority of the national economic development agenda and agriculture, the rural areas and farmers are also the top priorities of the government's work. In November 2012, the 18th National Congress of the CPC made it clear that by the year 2020, the modernization of agriculture and the construction of the new countryside must produce obvious effects as they are the prerequisites for a moderately affluent society. After years of hard work, China has freed itself from a long-term shortage of agriculture products and achieved a basic balance in supply and demand. Farmers are no longer suffering from shortages of food and clothing, and have become reasonably affluent. China has succeeded in feeding nearly 20% of the world's population with 9% of its arable land. This is not only a basis for China's further reform and opening up but also a great contribution to the development of mankind.

The decade since 2003 has witnessed the fastest development of China's agriculture and rural areas, from which Chinese farmers have benefited to an amazing extent. Grain production has gone up year after year. In 2012, the annual production increased to 589.57m tonnes from 430.7m tonnes in 2003, representing an annual average increase of 17.5m tonnes. Scientific and technological progress accounts for 54.5% of grain output growth; the total power of agricultural machinery reached one 1,000GW; integrated farming mechanization reached 57%; the penetration of improved grain varieties reached 96% and for the first time the grain yield per *mu* (about 0.0667 hectares) reached 350kg, which is responsible for 80.5% of the increase of total grain production. At the same time, the secondary and tertiary industries in the rural areas have developed with a strong momentum. The gross output of township enterprises exceeded Rmb6 trillion (US$897bn); the output value of agricultural product processing exceeded Rmb15 trillion (US$224bn); the total output value of agricultural reclamation surpassed Rmb500bn (US$74.7bn), and the total value of of agricultural product imports and exports surpassed US$170bn, in which exports amounted to US$65bn, reaching an all-time high.

The per capita net income of Chinese farmers has grown fast in recent years, rising from Rmb2,622 in 2003 to Rmb7,917 in 2012, with an annual increase of over Rmb540. It is gratifying that the growth in per capita net income of farmers has been higher than the growth of per capita disposable income of urban residents, promising to reduce the income gap between urban and rural residents. At the same time, the Chinese government has expedited the lifting of all constraints on farmers who want to find a job, to do business or to settle down in the cities. By the end of 2011, the total number of migrant workers in China exceeded 250m, of which over 30m have migrated with their families. Migrant farmers, also called migrant workers, have become the main source of labor in many industries in China. Such a massive flow of agricultural labor has fueled the commercial and industrial development in urban areas and contributed a lot to the socio-economic integration of urban and rural areas, creating new spaces for developing modern agriculture and promoting the income growth of farmers. Compared with 2002, the number of people employed in agriculture has dropped by over 70m in China, and the agricultural population in the rural areas has dropped by over 12%, giving each farmer another 20% or more of land for cultivation. In 2011, farmers' per capita income from salary was Rmb2,963.4 (compared with Rmb702.3 in 2000), accounting for 42.5% (31.2% in 2000) of the total per capita net income of farmers; farmers' per capita income from household business has increased by Rmb1,794.7 and its share of farmers' per capita net income has dropped by 17.2% over the same period. Farmers' income from salary has become a key driver in increasing their income in the 21st century.

Main Systems of China's Agriculture, Rural Areas and Farmers

Over the last decade, China has made great achievements in promoting agricultural and rural development and increasing farmers' incomes, primarily through implementing a series of policies aimed at strengthening agriculture, benefiting farmers and raising rural living standards. These incentives include: abolishing agricultural tax; deepening the reform of township institutions; providing direct subsidies for grain producers; setting minimum grain purchase prices; shifting the focus of infrastructure construction and social undertaking development to rural areas; ensuring rural compulsory education funds; running the new rural cooperative medical system; granting subsistence allowances in rural areas; running a new type of rural endowment insurance system; conducting collective forest tenure reform; making a clear commitment to keep existing land contract relationships stable and unchanged for a long time; raising subsidies for people living below the poverty line in rural areas by a big margin and giving classified guidance to the reform of the urban household registration system. The implementation of these policies which meet the real needs of Chinese farmers has greatly stimulated development momentum, creating a golden age for agricultural and rural development in China.

II. The Course of Structural Reform in Rural Areas
1. Background of reform

After the founding of the People's Republic of China (PRC) in October 1949, the Chinese government was faced with the problem of how to build socialism in a country with weak economic foundations. From 1949 to 1978, China learned from the Soviet Union and established a highly centralized planned economic system. It took 10 years to establish an independent and relatively complete industrial system and national economic system. However, as time passed, the highly centralized planned economic system could no longer meet the needs of the rapid development of China's economy and the country's fast-growing productivity. People's enthusiasm, initiative and originality were limited by this system, resulting in the loss of vitality and resilience in the socialist economy. The conflict between the national economic system and high productivity mainly manifested itself in China's rural areas, especially in the agricultural sector. The prevailing egalitarianism during the period of the people's communes (1958-1978) greatly dampened farmers' enthusiasm for production. Therefore, China's rural institutions had to be reformed to solve these problems at the roots and liberate the productive forces.

The 11th Central Committee of the CPC held its third plenary session in 1978, which lasted from December 18 to 22. Taking scientific stock of China's internal situation and prevailing global trends, and drawing on the experience and lessons of China and other countries in socialist construction, the CPC Central Committee decided to shift the focus of party and government work to socialist modernization. The strategy of 'reform and opening up' was adopted, which set China on a new course toward socialism. Reforms then started in the rural areas, including restoring and expanding the autonomy of rural communes and production brigades; allowing private plots, household sideline production, collective sideline production and rural trading; implementing the agricultural production responsibility system paying remuneration according to output; increasing the purchasing prices of grain and some other agricultural products; and adopting policy support for the development of a diversified economy. All these reforms have brought about remarkable changes in agriculture.

2. Progress of reform

After 30 years of continuous exploration and development, China's rural reform has proceeded through a series of trials and experiments featuring the gradual decentralization of agricultural policies, including local pilot programs and across-the-board implementation. Overall, China's rural reform has gone through three phases.

The initial phase of China's rural reform was the shift from the rural production and operational system to the household contract responsibility system, which started at the end of the 1970s. A basic rural economic system was established to safeguard farmers' autonomy in agricultural production, paving the way for later development of a market economy in China's rural areas. The second phase of China's rural reform was the market-oriented reform beginning in the mid-1980s, including the reform of the circulation system for agricultural products (to lift controls on the pricing and operation system of agricultural products) and ownership reform. Township enterprises could then be owned by individuals and joint households, not just people's communes and production brigades, and later the private economy grew on the basis of private ownership, which drove the development of diversifed economic sectors. Market-oriented reform in China's rural areas contributed a lot to the development of agriculture and the rural economy. The third phase of China's rural reform started in the early 21st century, aimed at formulating fundamental strategies to integrate economic and social development in urban and rural areas. The first reform was the change in the rural taxation system carried out step by step since 2000. Based on the regulation and integration of rural taxes and administrative charges, the central government first reduced agricultural tax rates, and then abolished all the four taxes on agriculture, namely agricultural tax, livestock slaughter tax, animal husbandry tax and tax on agricultural and forestry specialty products in 2006. Later state-owned farms were included in the rural tax system. As a result, the total tax burden on farmers was reduced by Rmb133.5bn. The central government also provided direct subsidies for grain producers, including direct grain subsidies, subsidies for purchasing superior crop varieties, subsidies for purchasing agricultural machinery and tools, and subsidies for purchasing general agricultural supplies. These subsidies totaled Rmb140.6bn by 2011. The grant of subsidies to farmers put an end to the regime of agricultural taxation in China that lasted 2,600 years and marked a new era of government subsidies for agricultural development. The reform of rural taxation was followed by the reform of agricultural product imports and exports. After China's accession to the World Trade Organization (WTO) in late 2001, China's agricultural sector was opened up to international investors, and China's agricultural products began to reach international markets. Third, the central government boosted general reforms targeting township institutions, compulsory education in rural areas and fiscal management systems at county and township levels. Fourth, the government also pushed forward the construction of a new socialist countryside and a new model of urbanization in accordance with the principle of coordinating urban and rural development.

Under the impetus of rural institutional reform, the dynamics and mechanisms of agricultural and rural development were also changed. There was a shift from a planned economy to a market economy where market mechanisms played an increasingly important role in agricultural and rural development. The methods and circumstances of agricultural and rural development were revolutionized, so a new type of farmer and modern technology were needed to develop a modern agriculture sector which would be able to participate in international competition. China's agricultural and rural development entered a new stage and the overarching goal is to comprehensively build a new socialist countryside and an affluent society.

Table 1-1: China's rural reform policy measures

Period	Key Policy Measures	Effects
1978-1984	Household contract responsibility system	Extraordinary development of agriculture
	Higher prices for agricultural products	Record-high grain output
	15-year term of land contracting	Rapid growth of farmers' incomes
1985-1999	Abolition of unified and fixed state purchase of agricultural products	Slowing down of agricultural growth
	Developing agricultural products market	Enlarged scope of agricultural market
	Adjusting rural economic structure	Diversified agricultural production
	Developing township enterprises	Diversified rural economic structure
	Instituting macroeconomic control	Slowing down of farmers' income growth
	Raising grain prices and intensifying reform of the circulation system	Accelerated agricultural production growth
	Establishing an agricultural market system	Changed supply and demand pattern for agricultural products
	30-year land contract system	Substantial rise in proportion of non-agricultural industries
	Rapid rise of township enterprises	Sharp rise of non-agricultural employment
	Liberalization of the household registration system and the emergence of 'migrant workers'	Rapid growth of farmers' incomes
2000 to date	Overall reform of rural taxation system	Abolition of agricultural tax
	Reform of agricultural products circulation system	China's agricultural sector open to international players
	Accession to the WTO	Restoration of growth of farmers' incomes
	Coordinating urban and rural development	All-round socio-economic development in China's rural areas
	Overall rural reforms and the construction of a new socialist countryside	Coordinated urban and rural economic development

Source: *30 Years of Rural Reform in China*, p2, Song Hongyuan, China Agriculture Press, March 2008.

III. Rural Land System and Basic Operational System
1. Rural land system

Article 2, Clause 1 of *The Land Management Law* of the PRC stipulates that China adopts and implements a socialist public land ownership system, namely, ownership by the whole people and collective ownership by the working people. According to this provision, land in China falls into two categories: land owned by the state on behalf of the whole people, and land collectively owned by farmers. According to Article 8 of the same law, land in urban districts is owned by the state, while land in rural and suburban areas (except when otherwise stated by law), including land reserved for house construction, and farmland and hills allocated to individual farmers for agricultural production, is collectively owned by farmers.

The land system plays a fundamental role in rural areas, underlying almost all other systems and institutions. It has a great influence on rural stability and social justice as it affects the allocation of land resources and land use efficiency. Since the reform and opening-up program started in the late 1970s, China has made great progress in defining and protecting farmers' land rights by increasing the market's role in allocating land resources, strengthening the protection of cultivated land, enhancing the state's control over land use, and improving the legal framework for land ownership. Yet despite the achievements, the land ownership system in rural areas is far from perfect. It still needs further reform to achieve better rural-urban integration, thus realizing the goals of scientific development. Guidelines for further reform are provided by the *Decision of the CPC Central Committee on Major Important Issues in Advancing Rural Reform and Development* (hereafter refered to as the Decision) issued at the third plenary session of the 17th CPC Central Committee in 2008. According to the Decision, further reform will carry on under the principles of clear ownership, land use control, economical and intensive use of land, and strict management.

(1) Establish systems to protect arable land and economical land use

Uphold strict protection of arable land. China is one of the countries with the biggest scarcity of land in relation to population in the world. To tackle the serious arable land shortage, the Chinese government has developed a series of strong protective policies regarding arable land in recent years to curb the trend of using cropland for urban construction, industrial park construction and other non-agricultural projects. Although these policies have had some effect, they have not substantially slowed down the conversion of agricultural land to non-agricultural purposes, mainly because of the massive demand for land for construction in both urban and rural areas, the lack of long-term compensation incentives for conserving arable land, and the illegal occupation of land. To safeguard the bottom line of preserving 1.8bn *mu* (120m hectares) of arable land, we must tighten control over land use and implement a stricter arable land protection policy. First, governments at every level must take responsibility for conserving arable land and basic farmland in their administrative districts. Second, the principles governing use of arable land for non-agricultural purposes are: compensation first followed by occupation;, maintenance of a general balance between occupation and compensation by not crossing provincial, district or municipal boundaries; preventing the tendencies of occupation without compensation, occupation before compensation or occupying more and compensating less and occupying superior land but compensating poorly. Third, basic farmland will be zoned nationwide to make sure that the total area of basic farmland does not shrink, basic farmland is not used for non-agricultural purposes, and the quality improves. For primary crop production areas which are given higher goals for arable land and basic farmland conservation, the state will put in place compensation mechanisms including economic incentives to mobilize local governments and farmers to protect cultivated land.

> **Basic farmland definition:**
>
> *Basic farmland is arable land that is not allowed to be converted to non-agricultural use for a very long period, and basic farmland conservation is a legally authorized administrative act to conserve basic farmland to meet the long-term demand for agricultural products due to population growth and the development of the national economy for a given period. Basic farmland to be conserved includes the following categories: arable land used for grain, cotton and oil-bearing crop production bases approved by the land administration department of the State Council or the local people's governments at and above the county level; high and stable yielding farmland; arable land with good water conservancy and water and soil conservation facilities, and medium and low-yield land where the execution of an improvement plan is in progress or medium and low-yield land that is transformable; vegetable production bases for large and medium-sized cities; experimental plots for research and teaching; and other arable land designated as basic farmland protection areas as stipulated by the State Council.*

Provisions on basic farmland protection are formulated in the 'PRC Land Management Law', the 'Regulations on the Protection of Basic Farmland', and other regulations issued by the PRC's Ministry of Land and Resources and the key regulations are as follows:

1. *Basic farmland protection planning system: People's governments at all levels will, in the process of compiling the overall planning for land utilization, list basic farmland protection as one of the contents of the planning, expressly defining the arrangements for the layout, quantitative targets and qualitative requirements of basic farmland protection.*

2. *Basic farmland protection zoning system: Zoning and demarcation of basic farmland protection zones should be carried out with the village (township) as the unit, organization for the implementation of which should be conducted by the relevant land administration department of the people's government at the county level in conjunction with the relevant department of agriculture administration at the same level.*

3. *Licensing system for occupation and use of basic farmland: No unit or individual can change or occupy basic farmland in a protection zone that has been demarcated in accordance with the law. In the event of inability to move away from basic farmland protection zones in site selection for such major construction projects as state energy, communications, water conservancy and military installations that require occupation of basic farmland involving diversion to other use of agricultural land or land requisition, it must be subject to the approval of the State Council. It is prohibited to occupy basic farmland by changing land use planning at any level of government.*

4. *Basic farmland occupation and compensation balancing system.*

5. *System to prohibit destruction or waste of basic farmland, or leaving it idle: Kiln building, house construction, tomb building, sand digging, quarrying, mining, earth gathering, piling up of solid wastes or other activities that destroy basic farmland by any unit or individual within basic farmland protection zones is prohibited. Occupation of basic farmland by any unit or individual for the development of forestry industry, fruit industry and digging of ponds for fish farming is prohibited. Leaving basic farmland idle or barren by any unit or individual is prohibited.*

6. *Basic farmland protection accountability system: This will be an important metric when evaluating the performance of government officials.*

7. *Basic farmland supervision and monitoring system: Local people's governments above the county level will establish a system of supervision and inspection to protect basic farmland, organize at regular intervals the relevant departments of land administration, agriculture administration as well as other departments concerned to conduct inspections for the protection of basic farmland and submit a report in writing of any problem discovered to the people's government at the next higher level.*

8. *Basic farmland local construction and environment conservation system: Relevant government departments of agriculture administration at all levels and contractors of basic farmland should take measures to fertilize the soil and protect farmland from being polluted.*

On 11 October 2012, the Ministry of Land and Resources held a video conference to promote the development of pilot counties to build high-standard basic farmland, requiring 500 pilot counties to accelerate the construction of high-standard basic farmland. During the 12th Five-Year Plan period (2011-2015), no less than 200m mu (13.3m hectares) of high-standard basic farmland (concentrated parcels of basic farmland with stable high yield which is resistant to natural disasters and meets the requirements of modern agriculture) is to be constructed, to ensure that the total area of high-standard basic farmland nationwide amounts to 400m mu (26.7m hectares).

The toughest policy will be enforced to promote economical land use. At present, uneconomical use or even waste of land is still a prominent problem in both urban and rural areas. As research results show, China's per capita land use for urban construction amounts to more than 130 square meters (sqm), higher than the average of 82.2sqm in developed countries and 83.3sqm in developing countries; the economic output of industrial land is far lower than the average of developed countries; and the use of land for construction in rural areas is very inefficient. To solve the conflict between conserving arable land and meeting the need for construction plots, we must make economical, intensive and efficient use of the existing land for construction rather than blindly expanding construction on green land. First, we must control the increase of land used for new construction projects. Second, we must make more efficient use of the existing construction land by integrating scattered construction land plots in urban areas, encouraging increased capacity and more intensive development of inefficiently used construction land, reforming non-urbanized areas in towns and cities, fast-tracking the transformation of urban ghettos, to increase land use efficiency and promote land-saving technologies and methods of construction. Third, we must explore new spaces for construction. On condition that the environment is not to be damaged, we must encourage development of uncultivated land and waste land, and promote use of vertical development and underground spaces.

(2) Protect farmers' rights to the contractual use of land, and improve the market for transfer of contractual operating rights

Farmers must be empowered to use land on the basis of contractual operation. The introduction of the household contractual responsibility system separated land use rights from collective land ownership. It is clearly stated in the Decision that the current land contract relationships should remain stable and unchanged in the long term, which is the basis of China's land system in the rural areas. Farmers have a strong desire for stable land rights. We must protect farmers' rights to occupy, use and benefit from contractual use of land. Reducing uncertainties in land contractual relationships is helpful to satisfy farmers' expectations in the long term.

The regulation of the transfer of contractual land use rights. The market for circulation of contractual land use rights has developed a lot since the late 1970s when China launched the reform program in rural areas which liberalized such transfers. After years' of trials, a system of policies, laws and regulations has been developed, including the principle of legal, voluntary and compensatory transfer, and different policy requirements for contractual land use right transfers in different periods. In line with previous policies, the *Decision* provides that farmers may transfer contractual land use rights in the form of subcontracts, leases, exchanges, assignments or joint-stock cooperation under the principle of legal, voluntary and compensatory transfers; areas where conditions are mature may develop various forms of moderately large-scale operation in forms such as big specialized household operations, family farms and farmers' professional cooperatives. The *Decision* also proposes 'three must nots' with regard to transfer of land operation rights: must not change the nature of collective ownership; must not change the land use; and must not harm farmers' land contractual rights and interests. To be more specific, collective farmers' ownership must not be changed into state ownership through transfer of contractual management rights or when a rural villager turns into a city dweller, and where the change of land ownership is necessary, it should go through certain legal processes. Farmland must be used for agricultural purposes only, and no individual or collective contractee may transfer or lease any agricultural land for any non-agricultural purposes. No individual or organization can seize or withhold the proceeds from the transfer of contractual land use rights which belong to farmers. No administrative means may be used to coerce contractual land use rights transfers; land circulation agencies should be tasked to better manage and facilitate the circulation of contractual land use rights.

In November 2014, a joint circular was issued by the General Office of the CPC Central Committee and the General Office of the State Council: *Opinions on Guiding the Systematic Transfer of Rural Land Operation Rights to Develop Appropriately Large-Scale Operations in Agriculture*. It points out that in the process of China's industrialization, informatization, urbanization and agricultural modernization, the development of appropriately large-scale operations in agriculture has become a general trend and the transfer of contractual land use rights is speeding up. Promoting the transfer of contractual land use rights and developing appropriately large-scale operations in agriculture have proved to be essential for building modern agriculture, as both can optimize the allocation of land resources, improve productivity, ensure food security and supply of the main agricultural products, promote new agricultural technologies, improve performance of agricultural operation and increase farmers' incomes. Yet the transfer of contractual land use rights and development of appropriately large-scale operations will be advanced in a prudent and smooth way, considering the large population and varied conditions across the vast rural areas of China.

To promote the transfer of contractual land use rights and development of appropriately large-scale operations, the following guidelines must be observed: First of all, a comprehensive modern agricultural operation system will be built on the basis of household operations, cooperation among households, enterprises and governments, and utilization of social intermediary services, and a modern agriculture system will feature modern Chinese characteristics including the application of advanced technologies, appropriately large-scale operations, strong competitiveness in the market, and friendliness to the environment. The system aims to achieve food security, increase agricultural output and promote the growth of farmers' incomes. The ownership rights, contractual land use rights and land operation rights will be separated. Household operations will be the fundamental form, while new operators will be cultivated and diverse forms of appropriately large-scale operations in agriculture will be developed. The development of appropriately large-scale operations will be aligned with the process of urbanization and labor migration from rural areas to urban areas, with the advancement of agricultural technologies and production means, and with the development of social intermediary services for agricultural operations. As a result, farmers must participate in and benefit from the transfer of contractual land use rights and the development of appropriately large-scale operations in agriculture.

The specific measures are as follows: First, the system of land contract operation rights in rural areas and contract relationships will be stabilized by improving the registration and certification of land contracts. Second, the transfer of land contract operation rights will be subject to better regulation through encouraging innovation in the method of transfer, and better supporting services for and control over the transfer of contractual rights will give effective support to large-scale grain production. Third, new forms of collective operation will be explored based on household operation through encouraging cooperation among households, and modern farming entities will be encouraged which can be run as enterprises, and therefore new business entities in agriculture will be cultivated through improved regulation and risk prevention. Lastly, diverse social intermediary services and up-to-date professional training for farmers will be provided and trading cooperatives will be utilized to establish a social service system.

(3) Promote land requisition system reform

In recent years, compensation for requisitioned land and requisition procedures have become more regulated thanks to local governments' land requisition reforms. Yet rather than creating benefits for farmers thus bridging the urban-rural gap in the process of urbanization and industrialization, land requisition has caused problems for farmers and enlarged the gap. The number of landless farmers is increasing due to large-scale land requisition. Social security and employment of landless farmers have become a tricky issue because of low requisition compensation. Therefore the *Decision* provides a solution to the problems by intensifying land requisition reform as follows:

Strictly defining the land for public good from that for commercial construction. It is provided in the constitution that the state may requisition land for public good with compensation in accordance with laws and regulations. Yet there is no clear definition on public good in laws and regulations such as *the Land Management Law*. Massive land requisitions in the name of public good have been used for commercial construction. According to the *Decision*, the scope of land subject to requisition will gradually be narrowed down by clearly defining the public good in land requisition. Farmers will be allowed to participate in and protect their legal rights and interests through various means in the process of the development and management of those non-public welfare projects with approval to use collective land in rural areas beyond the scope of land used for urban construction determined in the land use plan.

Establishing reasonable compensation rates and mechanisms. According to the *Land Management Law*, compensation for land requisition and labor resettlement are based on the average annual output value of the requisitioned land in the three years before requisition rather than on the location, socio-economic development and supply-demand relations in the requisitioned area, and the use and market value of the land after requisition, which leads to low compensation for farmers on requisitioned land. To improve the land requisition compensation mechanism, the *Decision* proposes to requisition collective land in rural areas according to law, make timely compensation for collective organizations and farmers in accordance with a unified standard, protect their information, participation, supervision and appeal rights, and develop a coordination and arbitration mechanism to provide legal assistance for land requisitioned from farmers in dealing with disputes over land requisition compensation problems.

Taking good care of the employment, housing and social security issues of farmers whose land has been requisitioned. Promote employment of farmers through various means such as providing professional training and produce favorable policies on loans, tax and sites for farmers whose land has been requisitioned seeking self-employment. Include the social security expenses of farmers whose land has been requisitioned into the compensation. Where the compensation cannot cover the expense, local governments should set aside money from their revenue on lending state-owned land use rights to fund it. Where social security issues affecting farmers whose land has been requisitioned haven't been solved, local governments should not approve the requisition. Where land requisition has surpassed a certain level, farmers may get some land for residential building and independent operation, on which they may develop projects to earn stable, long-term income.

(4) The system of residential building sites in rural areas

Residential building sites refer to plots of land used by farmers for the construction of their residences, including housing, accessories and courtyards. The land used for residential building sites in rural areas covers a very wide and large area, and is still increasing fast. Therefore the *Decision* provides for improvements in the residential building site system in rural areas by:

Regulating the management of residential building sites. The measures include: sticking to the policy of one residential building site per rural household; reorganizing the messy residential arrangements in rural areas to make it more orderly and concentrated, thus making economical use of land to facilitate infrastructure construction; encouraging farmers to build residences in a relatively concentrated way of their own accord on condition that their rights and interests are observed; renewing the decaying inner villages to make more efficient use of present residential building sites. The land saved from the reorganization and reform of present residential building sites will be reclaimed in the first place, and those earmarked for construction in compliance with land use plans will be put into the annual land use schedule of that year and prioritized to meet the needs of land for collective construction projects.

Protecting famers' usufructuary rights over residential building sites. A clearer definition of rights over residential building sites can better protect farmers' interests and fundamental habitat rights, which is also what farmers are expecting. Farmers' right to acquire, use and benefit from the land as residential building sites will be well protected through compensating farmers whose land for residential building gets requisitioned and prohibiting land requisitions against farmer's wills for non-agricultural purposes.

(5) The system of rural collective construction land

Rural collective construction land refers to the land used for building farmers' residences as well as manufacturing and service projects in rural areas, including construction land for the development of township enterprises, public facilities as well as for housing. At present, such land cannot circulate in the market because the land market in China is not sound or mature enough, and there is an obvious imbalance between urban and rural development. The *Decision* proposes to reform the system of rural collective construction land to create a unified construction land market in both urban and rural areas, which offers a very important policy direction for the reform of the system for collective construction land in rural areas. Such land entering the market on par with state-owned construction land may help develop a collective construction land price mechanism in rural areas which ensures equal rights and benefits for rural and urban areas, thus forming land prices that really reflect supply-demand relations in the market, and optimizing the allocation of land resources.

A unified construction land market is necessary for better regulation of the land market. Rural collective construction land blindly entering the market can be very disruptive, causing violations of rules, affecting land use planning, and resulting in ineffective control over total land supply. Therefore, regulating the trading of land will be a priority in the management of land resources in rural areas in the future. The *Decision* points out that the land acquired through legal transfer on the open unified land market will enjoy the same rights and benefits as state-owned construction land, as long as it doesn't violate government land use plans. The property value of rural collective construction land is becoming increasingly evident as China urbanizes and industrializes. Well regulated transfer of the utilization rights over rural collective construction land can help develop a unified construction land market accommodating orderly competition in both urban and rural areas, thus preventing political power from interfering with land prices and tapping the enormous economic potential of rural collective construction land.

2. Basic operation system for rural areas

(1) The establishment and development of a two-tier operation system

A two-tier operation system for the rural areas was established in the late 1970s during the agricultural reform based on household contract operations and the combination of centralization and decentralization. The two-tier operation system in agriculture is one of the most significant breakthroughs achieved in China's reform and opening up. In 1982, the basic principles of the household contract responsibility system were confirmed by the Central Government in its Document No. 1. In 1983, the household contract responsibility system was further defined as a two-tier operation system that combined unified collective operation and decentralized household operation in the Central Government's Document No. 1: *Several Problems in Current Rural Economic Policies*. In 1993, the household contract responsibility system and the two-tier operation system were added into the *Constitution* at the second session of the eighth NPC. In June of the same year, they were added into the Agriculture Law as amendments. In 2002, the household contract responsibility system was enhanced following the issue of the *Rural Land Contract Law of the PRC*. In 2007, the property attributes of the contractual operation rights of land were defined in the *Property Law*, which clearly defines farmers' contractual land operation rights. Over the past 30 years, the operation system in rural areas has become more and more enhanced and consolidated.

China's two-tier operation system in rural areas can be construed as follows. First, main production materials such as rural land are public or collectively owned. Land in rural and suburban areas, except where it is state-owned, is collectively owned by farmers, including residential building sites, private plots and private hill land. The rights of possession, use, usufruct and disposal over such land belongs to all farmers as a collective or, in some cases, in the form of rural collective organizations. Second, household contract operation is fundamental. It has been clearly provided for in the *Rural Land Contract Law* that China resorts to a system of contract operation of land in rural areas. Land in rural areas may be contracted to households in a collective, while land unsuitable for households to contract, such as land on barren mountains, valleys, hills and wasteland, may be leased out through bidding, auctions and public discussion. Third, China adheres to a two-tier operation system in rural areas. Unified collective operation and decentralized household operation are combined through contracts prescribing rights and responsibilities of all parties.

(2) Improvement of the basic operation system

During the past 30 years since the reform and opening-up program was launched in 1978, the basic operation system for rural areas has been maintained and greatly improved by the following means: First, industrialized operation of agriculture. The concept of industrialized operation of agriculture was put forward in the mid-1990s, aiming to transform the growth pattern of agriculture, create a channel connecting rural households to the market, and adapt agriculture to the market economy. By the end of September 2012, organizations of various kinds focusing on the industrialization of agriculture totaled 280,000, and more than 110m households were involved in the industrialized operation of agriculture, and their average annual income increased by Rmb2,400 (US$386). Second, professional cooperatives of farmers. Professional cooperatives are organizations established by farmers to hedge against risks as part of the market economy which started to take shape and went into operation in the 1980s. In 2007, *The Law of the PRC on Farmers' Professional Cooperatives* was enacted, which paved the way for and gave more potential to the development of farmers' professional cooperatives. There were more than 150,000 professional cooperatives at the end of 2008 involving more than 38.7m rural member households, accounting for 13.8% of all rural households in China and 55.12m non-member rural households were also involved as non-members. Usually one cooperative can comprise 100 to 200 households on average and the member households' average annual income can increase by about 20%, twice as high as the growth rate of common non-member households. Third, a social intermediary service system for agriculture. Such a system has an obvious advantage in solving problems which individual households cannot handle in the market. Currently, the system has been decentralized from government domination to involve multiple players including related government departments, agricultural enterprises and farmers' professional cooperatives. It covers various areas such as public welfare, mutual assistance and profit-seeking agricultural operation, and offers services before, during and after agriculture production. Fourth, innovation in forms of agricultural operation. Besides traditional household operation, new diversified forms of operation such as moderately large-scale operation, commissioned farmland operation and joint-stock (or equity-based) cooperative operation have also appeared as rural labor continues to transfer and the social service system for agriculture improves.

On the whole, the household contract system has proved to possess strong vitality through nationwide practice, and achieved enormous success in the following four dimensions:

Second, it has also helped optimize the rural employment structure. The two-tier operation system has given farmers who had been tied to the collective communes strong autonomy in making decisions concerning agricultural production. Along with the growth of township enterprises and the advancement of the secondary and tertiary sectors, a great amount of rural surplus labor has transferred to non-agriculture sectors and migrated into cities and towns, resulting in a tremendous change in the rural employment structure. In addition, it was so commonplace to have a part-time job that the workforce dedicated to agricultural production has been decreasing as a percentage of the total workforce and in terms of the absolute number of farmers as well. In 2012, the total number of rural migrant workers was 3.9% more than the previous year and rose to 262.61m, of which 163.36m migrant workers had migrated between provinces, and the remaining 99.25m had moved locally or within provinces, representing increases of 3.0% and 5.4% respectively.

Third, it has remarkably improved farmers' living conditions. The household contract responsibility system gave farmers the rights of autonomous operation and production on their farm land, which boosted their enthusiasm for production and helped increase their income substantially. Since the reform and opening up in the late 1970s, a continuous and rapid increase in farmers' incomes has drastically improved their living conditions. The per capita net income of farmers jumped from Rmb134 (US$21.50) in 1978 to Rmb7,917 (US$1,275.40) in 2012, and their per capita income rose at an average annual rate of 8% from 2004. China fulfilled the UN Millennium Development Goals objective of reducing the population living in extreme poverty by half ahead of the schedule (MDG 1), thus making an essential contribution to the global poverty reduction effort. China's rural population has made a historic leap from having no adequate food and clothing to leading a generally affluent life, and are now aiming at comprehensive affluence.

Fourth, it has advanced and improved a range of reform and opening-up policies. China's reform and opening up started in the rural areas, and agricultural reform started with household operation. On the basis of household contractual operations fully integrated with the establishment of the two-tier operation system, the highly centralized people's communes were brought to an end, releasing the potential of rural productive forces and boosting China's rural socio-economic development to a great extent, which was the basis of China's national development and prosperity in the following decades. Moreover, its implementation started China's march towards comprehensive reform and paved the way for China's economic system reform. It has led directly to the formation of a socialist market economy.

IV. Development of Township and Village Enterprises (TVEs)
1. The emergence of TVEs

Township and village enterprises (TVEs), then called 'commune and brigade enterprises', emerged in China in the mid-1950s. As a byproduct of the strategy of heavy industry priority in the 1950s, China played down the commune and brigade enterprises and strictly curbed their development, only allowing them to run local plants with local natural resources and materials, and to sell the products within the local area. In addition, the circulation of goods and transportation were prohibited, and no private businesses were allowed. The commune and brigade enterprises had hardly grown at all before China's reform and opening up in late 1978. There were

1.52m commune and brigade-run TVEs in China in 1978, averaging one TVE per 1,924 people in the rural areas. TVEs employed 28.27m farmers, accounting for 9.2% of the total rural workforce; and their gross output reached Rmb49.1bn (US$7.9bn), 7.17% of the national GDP and 24.1% of the output of the rural areas.

The fourth plenary session of the 11th Central Committee of the CPC, held in September 1979, adopted the *Decisions on Some problems in Speeding up the Development of Agriculture* in which the CPC and the government recognized the significant role TVEs could play in supporting rural economic development. Nevertheless, the development of TVEs was still impeded by the planned economy system. At that time, only collective enterprises were allowed and the distribution and pricing of TVEs' products were under strict government control. TVEs had no right to make managerial decisions, recruit employees and distribute profits. Some areas even went so far as to close down or suspend TVEs, and the number of TVEs decreased to 1,346,400 in 1983, lower than in 1978.

TVEs emerged as a new force to be reckoned with after 1984, however. With the nationwide adoption and implementation of the household co-production contractual responsibility system in China in 1983, agricultural productivity substantially improved and surplus labor in rural areas increased. The price of grain and sideline products shot up several times after 1978, which boosted farmers' incomes to an extent which allowed them to invest in their individual businesses. Meanwhile, farmers were becoming enthusiastic about setting up enterprises to further increase their income. They ran them either as part of collective enterprises or as independent enterprises, but both propelled the development of the rural economy. Under such circumstances, TVEs embraced rapid development. The number of TVEs surged to 6,065,200 by the end of 1984, 4,718,800 more than in the previous year, including 516,600 new village-run enterprises, and individual and private businesses started to boom. TVEs maintained a sound development momentum in 1985. There were 12,225,000 TVEs in China by the end of 1985, including 10,123,000 individual businesses run by farmers.

2. The development of TVEs

Along with the abolition of people's communes and production brigades in 1983, commune and brigade-run enterprises were renamed as TVEs, and cooperative, private and individual enterprises in which farmers had a stake were expanded according to a document issued by the Central Committee of the CPC and the State Council in March 1984. More importantly, this official document made it legally possible for farmers to own private businesses in individual names or groups.

From 1984 to 1988 was the most glorious period in the history of TVEs which increased dramatically in terms of their number, although the growth rate slowed down a bit. TVEs broke away from the restrictions in terms of ownership, businesses and industries. The original owners changed from communes and brigades to towns and villages and even individuals, and the portfolio of rural businesses expanded from production and trading of grain and relevant agricultural byproducts to a wide range including secondary and tertiary sectors such as manufacturing, commerce, transportation and construction. By 1988, the gross output of TVEs was equivalent to 24% of China's GDP and 58% of China's total rural output; and the employees working for TVEs accounted for 23.8% of the total rural labor force. TVEs paved the way for farmers to get rich and accounted for half of the rural economy.

However, the rapid development of TVEs gave rise to a collection of problems. What made things worse was that China suffered from severe inflation in 1989, which disrupted the national economy. The loans TVEs borrowed from the Agricultural Bank of China and rural credit cooperatives totaled Rmb84.786bn (US$13.6bn), which was five time higher than 1984 and strained those banks. Since TVEs lagged behind in technology, their rapid growth had been natural resources and energy intensive. The Chinese government started to adjust the economic system to restore economic order in 1989, which in turn led many TVEs to close down or transfer, and lots of employees lost their jobs and returned to the farmland. In a word, TVEs experienced hardly any growth between 1989 and 1991. Their development suffered a great setback.

TVEs recovered in 1992 and have boomed since then with the advances in economic system reform and the improvement of the macroeconomic environment. A series of reforms were conducted to redefine ownership and introduce new operational mechanisms for TVEs. TVEs also managed to improve their product quality, reduce their costs and increase their efficiency via technological development and talent acquisition and development. In an effort to bridge the development gap among TVEs in different regions, the Chinese government gave the less developed central and western regions special incentives to promote TVEs' development. In addition, the government strove to develop industry clusters in industrial parks or satellite towns. Scattered TVEs were integrated into clusters.

Therefore, China's TVEs experienced a second boom from 1992 to 1996. There were 23.36m TVEs employing a total of 135m workers in 1996, which was 1.2 times and 1.4 times higher than 1991 respectively. Farmers working for TVEs comprised 29.8% of the total rural workforce, which was 7.8% higher than 1991; and the gross output of TVEs was Rmb1.7659 trillion (US$284.4bn), 5.9 times more than in 1991. TVEs had become a major component of China's rural economy.

The *Law of the PRC on TVEs* was enacted on January 1, 1997 with the aim of facilitating the sound and sustained development of TVEs. The enactment of this law meant that the TVEs' rights and interests would be duly protected and also that they would operate under legal regulation. In the meantime, the TVE environment changed. China was plagued by commodity shortages for a relatively long period before 1998, whereas China's economy turned from a shortage (seller's) economy into a buyer's market with sufficient supply of commodities after 1998. There were also a wide range of other problems, like the lack of competitiveness on the part of smaller TVEs, the lack of managerial competence on the part of managers, and environmental pollution and depletion of resources caused by TVEs. In this context, rural enterprises were forced to accelerate their restructuring and systemic innovation starting from 1998 and focused on the following three aspects: their growth model shifted from extensive (externally driven) growth to intensive (internally driven) growth; the rapid increase in individual and private businesses diversified the ownership mix; and TVEs became a component of China's modern industrial system.

TVEs have profoundly altered China's rural economy landscape, which used to be mainly agriculture and grain production. The gross output of the former commune and brigade enterprises accounted for only 37% of the total agricultural output in 1978. After a decade's fast and sound development, the total output of TVEs in the secondary and tertiary sectors amounted to Rmb485.4bn (US$78.2bn) by the end of 1987, which exceeded the total output value of agriculture for the first time, accounting for104% of the total agricultural output. It was a milestone, indicating a bright prospect for China's rural development. The gross value of TVEs was 68.68% of the rural economy, which made TVEs a powerhouse in the rural economy of China.

The emergence and development of TVEs has revolutionized the development of China's rural economy and provided an immediate channel for deploying surplus rural labor. TVEs absorbed 2.416m of the surplus workforce in 2011, contributing to the optimization of the rural labor structure, alleviation of China's employment pressure and increase of productivity via scaled agricultural operation. Like the household contract responsibility system, TVEs were also key to the realization of affluence in rural China. In 2011, the wages TVEs paid their employees totaled Rmb59bn (US$9.5bn) and workers in TVEs earned annual incomes of Rmb24,420 (US$3,933), which boosted the farmers' goal of leading a better life.

However, there were also several bottlenecks restricting TVEs' development: disadvantaged geographical location in the rural areas; limited reform of ownership; backward technical equipment; shortage of managerial talent and technicians; limited access to financing due to small-scale operation; and underdevelopment in China's central and western regions. To make TVEs a cornerstone of the rural economy under such circumstances, the following measures will apply: further enhancing the reform of ownership to define property rights; attracting and retaining various competent professionals to quicken the technical transformation and innovation; optimizing the management mechanisms; bringing the scattered TVEs to key or central towns to form clusters or company groups with scale operation; and paying special attention to environmental conservation in the countryside.

V. The Governance Structure of Towns and Villages

1. 'Town government and village administration' since the start of reforms

With the start of economic reform in 1978, specifically the adoption of the household contract responsibility system in the rural areas, the collectivized land system dissolved and farmers regained their autonomy in production and distribution of goods. The people's commune system gradually dissolved, too, and lost its power, leading to dramatic changes in rural governance at town and village level.

The so-called 'town government and village administration' consists of two levels: 'town government' and 'village administration'. 'Town government' is the lowest level of government in China governing the rural areas on behalf of the state, while 'village administration' is an autonomous body governed by a villagers' committee which practices democratic elections, democratic decision-making, democratic management and democratic supervision. Town government embodies state power whereas village administration is the embodiment of social rights and power. The former is the predominant power while the latter is the foundation for the exercise of power. In particular, the above-mentioned two local organizations are different in four aspects: the nature of power, the structure of power, the execution of power and the hierarchy of power.

First, in terms of the nature of power, given that the Chinese constitution stipulates that all power in the PRC belongs to the people, the state power exercised by town government offices and the autonomous power belonging to village administration all rest with the people. Evidently, they share the same source of power but are quite different in nature. Town government represents the extension of state power into the rural areas, whereas village administration represents the vigorous growth of social power. The relationship between town government and village administration is the relationship between state government power and grassroots social power. This is also an important difference between the structure of town government and village administration, and that of the people's commune system.

Second, in terms of the structure of power, the town is the lowest level of government in the countryside, its organ of power is the town people's congress, the town government is the executive organ of its power, and the town party committee exercises unified leadership of the town people's congress and the town government. On the other hand, village administration provides autonomy for the grassroots masses of farmers, the decision-making organ of its power is the village council or village representative council, the executive organ of its power is the village committee, and the village party branch is the core of grassroots leadership and gives prominence to the party's unified leadership.

Third, in terms of the exercise and operation of power, a town, as the representative of state power, exercises state power over the rural areas pursuant to the constitution, and is obliged to carry out the administrative orders and regulations of the central government within its local jurisdiction. Thus, it becomes a local implementer of state policy. Meanwhile, as an autonomous body, a village committee is formed through democratic election, adopts democratic decision-making processes, implements democratic management, and is subject to democratic supervision. Along with two vice chairmen and other members of the village committee, the chairman of the village committee is elected by the villagers; and villagers also take the initiative in discussing and handling the management of the village and formulating the village regulations. The autonomous village committee is indeed an embodiment of the power of the villagers.

Fourth, in terms of the purpose of the exercise of power, a town, at the lowest level of the state government hierarchy, assumes the responsibility of enforcing government policies to fulfill the tasks and goals imposed by its higher authorities. It is basically responsible to the higher authorities. However, a village committee is beyond the realm of state governance. A village committee is responsible to the individual villagers. It is organized via direct democratic election by the villagers by which they manage their own affairs, educate themselves and serve their own needs.

Local governance consisting of 'town government and village administration' is a unique administrative model for China's rural areas, conceived by the upper levels in China to serve the development of the socialist market economy with its distinct feature of socialism with Chinese characteristics. A town government is a centralized administrative body exercising state power; a village committee is an autonomous mass organization based on common regulations and equal rights of villagers in decision-making concerning the management of village affairs. So when one talks of village administration with respect to town government, village administration is the cornerstone., 'Town government and village administration' is a defining characteristic of China's rural politics.

2. Exploring new mechanisms of local governance

In the new historical period, China's rural governance has entered a new phase of development. To facilitate the construction of harmonious rural communities, the grassroots organizations must play a more positive role and optimize their potential by exploring new local governance mechanisms and redefining the relations between, including the rights, duties and limitations of, various governance bodies. The following measures need to be enforced to create synergy among all related sectors:

First, the relationships between town and village governments and village committees must be redefined by law, to enhance the relevant legal system. Enacted in 1998, *The Village Committee Organization Law* established that a village committee is the primary autonomous mass organization, and should operate under the guidance of the town and assist the town government in its work. On this basis, the pertinent regulations must be developed and specified so as to further define the limits of power between the town government and the village committee, and also to clarify the means and the extent to which a town should guide the work of a village committee and a village committee should assist the work of a town.

Second, further improvements should be made to the mechanisms governing the autonomy of village committees to enhance their autonomous capabilities. A village committee plays a significant role in rural autonomy. As a mass autonomous organization, the village committee is a governance body organized by the villagers themselves in which the villagers manage their own affairs, educate themselves, and serve their own needs, which stimulates the villagers' enthusiasm to deal with their own affairs. The key to improving the autonomy of village committees is to clearly define the responsibilities and work procedures of the CPC branch in the village and the village committee, which means seeking a coordinated and sound relationship between CPC leadership and villagers' autonomy.

Third, it is imperative to advance town government reform and to improve local governance to suit the rapid development and changes in rural areas. As China seeks new mechanisms of rural governance in the construction of a new countryside, it is important to transform a town government from a management-model into a service model of government; a town should be mainly responsible for facilitating the advancement of social undertakings and the construction of a harmonious society. Its focus should rest on enhancing public services and social administration. A town should transfer its operative, community and social services to non-government agencies. For instance, a town could adopt market-oriented methods such as bidding and tendering, contracting, renting, and charging to encourage private organizations to perform public services and social administration.

Fourth, support and incentives should be given to boost the development of rural social service organizations. Rural social service organizations in China have remained underdeveloped, since the vast majority of villagers are not well organized and therefore lack the institutional access to participate in village autonomy. Except for those villagers who are elected as delegates to the people's congresses or party congresses, or members of the village committee, villagers have limited opportunities to voice their opinion on certain public affairs concerning their own village. In the less developed areas, village enterprises are too small to support the rural economy, which in turn creates an illusion that the town is mainly responsible for the local economic growth. With the industrialization of agriculture and development of the market economy, farmers increasingly need to set up and join organizations to secure their interests and hedge against market risks. The ultimate goal is for villagers to realize self-management, self-education, and self-service, and to make them the key players in rural governance.

Over 98% of 589,000 Village Committees in China's Rural Areas Practice Direct Elections

On March 13, 2013, a press conference was held at the Media Center by the Press Center of the First Session of the 12th National People's Congress.

In answer to a question on China's democracy at the village level, Jiang Li, Vice Minister of Civil Affairs, noted that "democratic election of village committees is the most common practice in the socialist politics with Chinese characteristics among Chinese villagers. By the end of 2012, some 589,000 village committees had been established throughout the country, and most of the provinces, autonomous regions and municipalities directly under the central government had elected their eighth or ninth committees. What's more important is that 98% of the village committees have been directly elected and the average participation rate of villagers in such elections is above 95%. The latest round of direct elections for village committees started in 2011, and will conclude by the end of this year. In terms of voters, it will become the most widely participated-in election anywhere in the world: there will be 600m participants. The process involves secret ballots and open vote-counting, with secret ballot booths being very common, villagers are now able to elect their village committees in accordance with their own will. Democratic elections have become an important part of community-level democracy in rural China while, of course, village self-government also includes democratic decision-making, democratic management, and democratic supervision. Grassroots political democracy will become a reality when the above four practices are fully implemented in rural areas.

Chapter 2

How to Promote the Modernization of China's Agriculture

As a developing country with the biggest population in the world, China's per capita share of natural resources, especially agricultural resources, is inadequate. In China, the per capita arable land is 1.38 *mu* (0.092 hectare), per capita fresh water is 2,134 cubic meters (in 2007), and per capita forest is 10.2sqm (2012), which represents respectively 40%, 33% and 11% of the world average; and per capita grassland is 33% of the world average.

Thanks to the advancement of comprehensive rural reform, including the nationwide adoption and implementation of the household contract responsibility system since 1978, the establishment and improvement of the socialist market economy. and the deepening of reform and opening up, China has improved the efficiency of its agricultural resource allocation and optimized the structure of crop cultivation, and therefore the overall productivity of agriculture has risen notably and grain output has been drastically increased to 400m tonnes, then to 500m tonnes, which boosted China's domestic food availability from being in short supply to being in balanced supply, making China self-sufficient in grain supply for its people. China has seen an unprecedented level of growth and improvement in the agricultural sector since the beginning of the 21st century, mainly in the development of modern agriculture and radical changes in the mode of production in agriculture. Over the last decade, agricultural machinery has been widely applied, quality seed and good agricultural practices have been promoted, and the management of grain production has steadily improved in China. Quality seed coverage for major grain crop varieties exceeds 96%, and the increase in per unit area yield has contributed over 80% to overall growth in the total grain output. Technology has become a strong boost for agricultural development, and the contribution of technology to agricultural growth reached 54.5% in 2012, which was 6.5 percentage points higher than in 2006. China's agricultural machinery has also been promoted in most grain producing areas, and its agricultural mechanization rose to 57%, which was 19 percentage points up from 2006. China has seen a great change in agricultural production from dependence on human power and animal power to mechanization.

Table 2-1: China's Major Agricultural Product Output (unit: million tonnes)

Year	Grain (Cereals, beans, potatoes)	Oil-bearing products	Cotton	Fruit	Meat	Dairy products	Aquatic products
2001	452.637	28.649	5.324	66.580	60.139	11.229	37.959
2002	457.058	28.972	4.916	69.520	61.058	14.004	39.549
2003	430.695	2.811	4.860	145.174	64.433	18.486	40.770
2004	469.470	30.659	6.324	153.409	66.087	23.684	42.466
2005	484.022	30.771	5.714	161.201	69.389	28.648	44.199
2006	498.039	30.594	6.746	172.399	70.890	33.025	45.836
2007	501.600	24.610	7.600	181.363	68.657	36.334	47.475
2008	528.710	29.528	7.492	192.202	72.787	37.815	48.956
2009	530.820	31.543	6.377	203.955	76.499	36.777	51.164
2010	546.477	32.301	5.961	214.014	79.258	37.480	53.730
2011	571.208	33.068	6.589	227.682	79.578	38.107	56.032

Source: China Statistical Yearbook 2012, China Statistics Press

Table 2-2: China's world ranking by major agricultural products

Agricultural products	1978	1980	1990	2000	2007	2008	2009	2010
Cereals	2	1	1	1	1	1	1	1
Meat①	3	2	1	1	1	1	1	1
Cotton	3	3	1	1	1	1	1	1
Soybeans	3	3	3	4	4	4	4	4
Peanuts	2	2	2	1	1	1	1	1
Rapeseed	2	2	1	1	1	2	1	1
Sugar cane	7	9	4	3	3	3	3	3
Tea	2	2	2	2	1	1	1	1
Fruit②	9	10	4	1	1	1	1	1

Source: FAO statistics
Notes:
① Before 1990, the ranking was measured by the output of Pork, Beef, and Mutton.
② Excluding melon plants.

> **China sees 11th consecutive bumper harvest (2003-2014)**
>
> *[Xinhua, Beijing, December 4, 2014] Data from the National Bureau of Statistics (NBS) show that China witnessed an 11th consecutive year of growth in its grain harvest in 2014. With an increase of 5.16m tonnes, up 0.9% from the previous year, China's grain output totaled 607.099m tonnes.*
>
> *According to the NBS, with a growth of 4.577m tonnes, up 0.8% from the previous year, the main crop yield reached 557.269m tonnes in 2014, including maize, grain, wheat, barley, Chinese sorghum, buck wheat and oats.*
>
> *According to the sample survey among farmers and investigation of agricultural producing organizations by the NBS throughout China's provinces, municipalities and autonomous regions, the total area for grain cultivation was 112.7383m hectares (1.691074bn mu), 0.7% up from the previous year; and the average grain output was 5,385tonnes/hectare (t/ha), 0.2% higher than 2013.*

Source: *Farmer's Daily*, December 10, 2014

http://www.farmer.com.cn/newzt/sylz/gz/201412/t20141210_1000395.htm

Due to the ever increasing market demand and the constraints of natural resources and the environment on agricultural production, it is essential for China to transform its agricultural development model and promote sustainable modernized agriculture in the coming years. According to the 12th Five-Year Plan (2011-2015), China will promote industrialization, urbanization, and agricultural modernization simultaneously. The development of modern agriculture is a key step to transform the model of economic development and build an affluent society; it is also an inevitable step in building a new socialist countryside in China through increasing overall agricultural productivity and farmers' incomes.

I. Safeguarding National Food Security

At the Central Conference on Rural Work in December 2013, Chinese President Xi Jinping stressed the strategic importance and pointed out the direction of deepening rural reform to sustain long-term sound and steady economic growth and social development. The meeting also put forward the specific objectives of China's rural reform and stressed that to build a moderately prosperous society, the key is to improve the living standards of farmers, which is based on the fact that agricultural modernization has lagged behind in China's Four Modernizations and become a hurdle in China's progress towards a better-off society. Furthermore, the meeting noted that "a strong agricultural sector is the prerequisite for a strong China, a beautiful countryside is the prerequisite for a beautiful China and better-off farmers are the prerequisite for a prosperous China". By sticking to the long-term principle of industry supporting agriculture and the urban areas supporting the rural areas, and by means of a series of supportive policies and measures to boost rural development, China will continue to put agriculture, farmers and rural areas on the top of its agenda and prioritize the advancement of agriculture, farmers and rural areas.

The meeting communique also noted that food security for the country's enormous population is the first and foremost challenge facing China. The bowls of the Chinese, in any situation, must rest soundly in our own hands, so to speak. Our bowls should be filled mainly with Chinese grain. When a country is basically self-sufficient in food supply, it can grasp the overall situation for socio-economic growth. Hence, it is vital to stick to a national food security strategy based on domestic supply, which relies on increased production capacity and advanced science and technology, and moderate imports. And the following measures, which are the focal points in ensuring self-sufficient food supply and adequate food storage, are essential and should be implemented: stabilize the grain producing areas, and maintain the existing arable land area at not less than 1.8bn *mu* (120m hectares) to safeguard the existing arable land area against any decrease; stimulate and protect the 'two enthusiasms' of farmers to produce food, and motivate the main food production areas to increase grain output at the same time; maintain a reasonable level of food storage and guarantee proper food distribution in case of emergency, for which the central government will assume the main food security responsibility, and work together with provincial and town-level governments to provide financial aid for grain production; make better use of domestic and foreign markets and resources, keep imports stable and accelerate the pace of agricultural globalization; and advocate economical consumption of food, increase public awareness of the need to conserve food and make it a common practice nationwide.

The central government has made it clear that China will keep cereals basically self-sufficient and staple foods absolutely secured. Given the availability of natural resources, China will focus on maintaining self-sufficiency in the main grain products; and it is important to note that it is impossible to rely on the international market to feed China's huge population. Largely because international grain prices are lower than the domestic market, however, China has increased its grain imports in recent years to meet the diversified demand of its population for food products. Imports of three main grains - rice, wheat and corn - account for a meager 2.4% of the total domestic grain output. China will continue to import several food varieties that are in short supply domestically in the future. On the other hand, insisting on China's self-sufficient food security strategy and taking into consideration farmers' employment so as to increase their income, China will not sharply increase its import of grain products.

China will take the following measures to significantly increase domestic grain production:

1. Stabilize the land area sown to grain. We must protect arable land, especially basic farmland, control the use of agricultural land for non-agricultural purposes, and expand arable land through land reconsolidation and reclamation to ensure that the total arable land is no less than 1.8bn *mu* (120m hectares) and the soil resilience has been regenerated. In order to maintain the cultivated land at no less than 1.56bn *mu* (104m hectares), including 475m *mu* (31.7m hectares) of rice fields, China has been working to demarcate basic farmland conservation areas throughout the country. China is also working hard to select a number of arable and productive grain production bases for permanent conservation. In addition, it is important to raise the potential multiple cropping index to safeguard a steady arable land area of over 1.6bn *mu* (106.7m hectares), including a stable grain land area of 1.26bn *mu* (84m hectares).

2. Optimize the mix of grain varieties. China will optimize grain production according to local geological and climate conditions in different regions of China: by promoting double-cropping rice production in southern China; by expanding the growing area of quality Japonica rice in northeastern China; by gradually replacing Indica rice with Japonica rice in the area between the Yangtze River and the Huai River; and by encouraging the cultivation of quality wheat for specific end-use. At the same time, we will expand the corn planting acreage to cultivate quality corn for specific end-use; encourage farmers to produce more high-oil and high-protein soybeans to ensure China's self-sufficiency in soybeans; increase the production of coarse grains and promote the cultivation of quality varieties of potatoes.

3. Increase the per unit area yield of grain. China will select quality new grain varieties and speed up their propagation and cultivation so as to improve the cultivation ratio of quality seed for grain production. We will transform traditional agricultural practices and employ new methods to develop China's agricultural mechanization in a professional and systematic manner, including the application of industrialized seedling nurturing and greenhouse seedling nurturing. The practice of deep ploughing to loosen and turn over the soil on arable land will be promoted which is helpful for alleviating soil compaction and improving crop yields. High-yield cultivation technologies, such as the use of sowing seeds without ploughing and formula fertilization after soil testing, will also be promoted. And local land and climate conditions in different regions will be taken into account to ensure large-scale sustainable food increases.

With the rapid advancement of industrialization and urbanization, China's natural resources have been strained and farmland contamination has been aggravated. Taking all these circumstances into consideration, the central government, especially the authority responsible for agriculture, is adopting decisive measures to protect and improve the quality of arable land. The overall goal is to develop high-quality farmland through improving rural agricultural facilities; to raise the soil fertility of cultivated land to a new level - 0.5% higher - by 2020, and to increase the content of organic matter in the soil by 0.5% as well; and to upgrade the quality of cultivated land to effectively avert any further increase in acid land, saline-alkali land and farmland contaminated by heavy metals via: enriching soil fertility to enhance water and nutrient conservation; curbing the overuse of chemical fertilizers and pesticides; and reducing organic matter accumulation in heavy metal-contaminated farmland soil. Under huge pressure to fix its worsening farming environment, China will formulate guidelines to improve the quality of arable land in different regions with specific solutions; setting national standards for upgrading the quality of arable land; protecting the existing arable land properly in accordance with *The Regulations on the Protection of Basic Farmland*; and demarcating basic farmland preservation areas all over the country.

A tiny rice seed changes the world

The UN's World Food Program (WFP) executive director James Morris told reporters while he was in Beijing for a two-day visit that the UNWFP would end food aid to China by the end of 2005. The UNWFP said its 26-year program of food aid to China would officially stop from 2006 onwards, and called on Beijing to play a bigger role as a global donor. Since the hybrid rice developed by Yuan Longping was planted all over China, China has been able to feed its population, which is 20% or more of the world's total, with less than 10% of the world's total arable land.

In 1973, together with his teammates, Yuan Longping successfully cultivated a type of hybrid rice species which had great advantages. The new hybrid rice type has been grown on half of the country's rice fields since then, ensuring a sufficient food supply for over one billion Chinese and forcefully answering the question of 'who will feed China'.

At a national conference on hybrid rice held in October, Yuan Longping circulated a paper entitled Utilization of 'Wild-Abortive-type (WA)' Seed Selection 'Three-Line System' of Development and unveiled the first successfully bred 'three-line system' of Indica hybrid rice species.

In 1976 China started large-scale planting of hybrid rice, with the total area sown to three-line hybrid rice reaching 2.08m mu (138,666.7 hectares), with an increase in output of over 20%. For this huge contribution, Yuan Longping was granted new China's first National Top-Grade Invention Award in 1981.

In 1982, at an academic conference of the International Rice Research Institute, renowned Chinese scientist Yuan Longping, was for the first time publicly acknowledged as the world's 'father of hybrid rice'.

In 1986, he further proposed a strategy for breeding hybrid rice with a step-by-step method to gradually develop three-line, two-line and super hybrid rice. His method was accepted as part of China's National 863 Program, and he was appointed head of a research team comprising 16 partners from all over China. Two-line hybrid rice was planted nationwide in 1995, contributing to an average annual increase of 5% to 10% over the three-line system.

Soon afterwards, Yuan pointed out that it was necessary to carry out the heroic task of developing super hybrid rice in phases, and advocated a new technology which could effectively improve the photosynthesis effect by combining selected quality seed with hybridization.

In 2000, the objective of producing 10.5t/ha (700kg/mu) for Phase I super rice was attained, and the Phase II objective of 12t/ha (800kg/mu) was accomplished in 2004. A Phase III super rice breed developed under Yuan's guidance yielded 13.5t/ha (900kg/mu) in a small-scale pilot field in 2005.

The introduction and development of hybrid rice ended the food shortage in China, and also provided an essential solution for reducing worldwide starvation. From Asia to America and even as far afield as Africa and Europe, this super-yield hybrid rice was nicknamed 'oriental magic rice', 'giant rice', 'waterfall rice', and is even ranked alongside ancient China's four major inventions (papermaking, printing, the compass and gunpowder).

Yuan has received a list of awards for his innovative contributions in developing hybrid rice, such as the Wolf Prize for Agriculture and the World Food Prize in 2004. He was also elected as a foreign associate of the US National Academy of Sciences in 2006.

Source: Xinhua Net, 25 August 2009

http://news.sina.com.cn/c/2009-08-25/175918508894.shtml

China's father of hybrid rice: Yuan Longping

Yuan Longping, born on September 7, 1930 in Beijing, now lives in Changsha (capital city of Hunan Province). He is an expert in hybrid rice breeding. He is highly acclaimed as the father of hybrid rice for his enormous contributions to the development of hybrid rice. He is also a member of the Chinese Engineering

Academy. He was elected as a foreign associate of the US National Academy of Sciences in 2006, received an honorary doctoral degree from Macau University of Science and Technology in 2010, and won Malaysia's Mahathir Science Award in 2011.

Currently, he is a member of the Standing Committee of the 12th National Committee of the Chinese People's Political Consultative Conference (CPPCC), and also vice chairman of the CPPCC Hunan Provincial Committee and of the Hunan Provincial Association for Science and Technology. He is the director general of the China National Hybrid Rice Research & Development Center and Hunan Hybrid Rice Research Center. He is also the honorary dean of several colleges in China, including the College of Agronomy and Biotechnology of China's Southwest University in Chongqing, Huaihua Vocational and Technical Collage and Hunan Biological and Electromechanical Polytechnic. He is a professor at Hunan Agricultural University and a visiting professor at China Agricultural University. He also acts as chief consultant for the UN's FAO. In addition, he is an honorary president of the 1st World Chinese Association of Healthy Eating.

4. Enhance the development of major grain producing regions. Major grain producing provinces, cities and counties are the vital elements in ensuring China's food security. China's 13 major grain producing provinces account for 75% of the national total in terms of output, 80% in terms of grain circulation in the market, and 90% in terms of transport to other areas. More than 400 major grain producing counties claim a grain output of more than 1bn *jin* (500,000 tonnes) which accounts for 54% of the total national output, and 33 major cities (prefecture-level cities) produce a grain output of over 10bn *jin* (5m tonnes), and their combined output accounts for 43% of the national total. The major agricultural regions constitute an essential 'safety net' for China's food security.

A total of 800 major grain-producing counties have been identified as the key areas in planning to build more than 100bn *jin* (50m tonnes) of grain production capacity. We will increase investment, speed up the development of new production capacity and build core grain-producing areas and major grain-production counties in non-core areas into stable high-yield commercial grain-production bases. On the premise of protecting the ecological environment, we will develop food production reserves when appropriate depending on the overall grain supply and demand situation.

Yushu Municipality, Jilin Province: planned construction as a major grain-producing area

Yushu Minicpality in Jilin Province is one of the important commodity grain-producing bases in China and is described as "the greatest bread-basket in China". In 2010, Yushu Municipality was listed as one of the first 50 modern agricultural demonstration zones.

In 2011, the city's agricultural area reached 379,000 hectares, of which 347,000 hectares was sown to grain. In 2011, the city's grain output reached 6.2bn jin (3,100m tonnes), hitting an all-time high and winning for Yushu the title of "the national grain production pacesetter county (city)" for eight consecutive years. The municipal government has implemented scientific planning of its demonstration zone construction, including developing one-million-mu high-standard farmland, overall mechanization, developing a vegetable production base, facilitating an animal husbandry industry production base and agricultural industrialization.

1. *Yushu Municpality has vigorously promoted land scale management, on the condition that the land ownership remains unchanged. In 2011 the city's land circulation area reached 870,000 mu (58,000 hectares), and it fostered 500 large-scale grain production households, incubated 436 farmer entrepreneurs and set up 330 farmers' cooperation organizations.*

2. *Yushu Municipality has promoted mechanization of farming and introduced a large amount of advanced equipment. The city had 28,510 vehicles, of which 13,493 were large tractors. And the city's agricultural mechanization level stood ahead of other parts of China.*

3. *Yushu Municipality has developed irrigation works and added water-conservation irrigation facilities to 100,000 mu (6,667 hectares) of farmland in order to increase grain yield. The municipality has realized high-density corn planting, which could raise the yield by 30%.*

4. *Relying on agricultural science and technology, Yushu Municipality has collectively put agricultural funds into the construction of high-standard farmland, investing Rmb45m (some US$7,22m) into the construction of 410,000 mu (27,333 hectares) of high-yield demonstration farmland. The municipality has promoted synthetic technical measures to increase yields including: formula fertilization after soil testing; adopting conservation-oriented ploughing technology; planting maize in wide and narrow rows*

allowing some land to lie fallow;.destroying farmland rodents; and achieving widespread coverage of Trichogramma wasps to control crop damage by Asian corn borer insects.

5. *Continue to expand construction of northern China's winter vegetable production base. In all, 26 new vegetable parks have been built and 1,440 solar greenhouses as well as 1,560 normal greenhouses, bringing the total number to 44,000, and total vegetable production was worth Rmb1.8bn (US$290m). The municipality aims to basically raise the average greenhouse ownership to one per household within 10 years, turning Yushu Municipality into a 'northern Shouguang' (Shouguang Municipality is a renowned vegetable production base in Shandong Province).*

5. To improve the incentive mechanisms for encouraging food production. We will establish and perfect a compensation mechanism for the major grain-producing areas, including encouraging policies and measures to support major grain-producing areas. We will also strengthen the incentive measures for major grain-producing counties, linking fiscal support to grain-growing areas, grain yield, grain circulation in the market and the amount of grain transported to other areas. The funding for county-level agricultural infrastructure construction will be phased out for major grain-producing counties. Instead, a grain subsidy system will be established, and concrete measures of granting direct subsidies according to the grain growing area, grain yield and the amount of grain sold to the state will be explored, to fully and most effectively stimulate grain production and ensure farmers' benefits.

In order to encourage the use of rural land for grain production, the *Opinions on Guiding the Transfer of Rural Land Operation Rights and Encouraging Moderate-Scale Agricultural Management* was issued by the State Council in November 2014. This provides that first, new subsidies will be granted to scale grain production operators; second, land operators will be encouraged to participate in food production by means of a sectoral planning for the major grain-producing areas, functional grain-producing areas and creative high-yield project areas and relative supporting policies; third, we will keep the land-transfer price at a reasonable level, thus reducing the food production costs and stabilizing the grain area planted to grain.

II. Promote Strategic Restructuring of Agriculture

1. Optimizing the arrangement of agricultural regions. At the planning level, China will tailor measures to suit local conditions and give full play to the advantages of each area. We will encourage and support advantageous areas to focus on planting grain, cotton, oilseed, sugar crops and other staple agricultural products. We will strengthen the construction of bases for vegetables, fruit, tea, flowers, silkworm cocoons and other horticultural products, and develop livestock and aquatic production zones with distinctive features of their own. We will accelerate the establishment of a strategic arrangement of agriculture comprising 'seven zones and 23 belts', with the Northeast Plain, North China Plain (also known as the Yellow River, Huai He and Hai He River Basin), Yangtze River Basin, Fen River-Wei River Plain, Hetao Irrigation Area, South China, Gansu and Xinjiang as the main agricultural production zones, with other agricultural areas as important components.

> ***China maps out strategic arrangements for agriculture comprising 'seven zones and 23 belts'***
>
> *According to The National Master Plan for Functional Zoning issued by the State Council in late 2010, China will establish strategic arrangements for agriculture comprising 'seven zones and 23 belts'.*
>
> *'Seven zones and 23 belts' refers to the seven main agricultural production zones and 23 agricultural products including wheat, maize and cotton. The seven zones are: the Northeast Plain, North China Plain, Yangtze River Basin, Fen River–Wei River Plain, Hetao Irrigation Area, South China, Gansu and Xinjiang, in which basic farmland is the basis, and the other agricultural areas are important components.*

> The Northeast Plain will build high-quality rice, special corn, soybean and livestock belts.
>
> The North China Plain will build high-quality special wheat, high-quality cotton, special corn, soybean and livestock belts.
>
> The Yangtze River Basin will build high-quality rice, high-quality special wheat, high-quality cotton, oilseed rape, livestock products and aquatic belts.
>
> The Fen River-Wei River Plain will build high-quality special wheat and special corn industry belts.
>
> The Hetao Irrigation Area will build a high-quality special wheat belt.
>
> South China will build high-quality rice, sugar cane and aquatic belts.
>
> Gansu and Xinjiang will build high-quality special wheat and high-quality cotton belts.
>
> In addition, we will also actively support the development of other agricultural zones and other characteristic agricultural products with advantages, which need the necessary policy guidance and support from the state according to their specialty. These agricultural products and belts include: the Southwest and Northeast China wheat belt, the Southwest/Southeast China corn belt, South China's high-protein soybean and vegetable soybean belt, North China's oilseed rape belt, Northeast, North, Northwest, Southwest and South China's potato belts, Guangxi, Yunnan, Guangdong and Hainan Provinces' sugarcane belts, Hainan, Yunnan and Guangdong Provinces' natural rubber belts, Hainan's tropical agricultural product belts, coastal regions' pig belt, Northwest China's beef and mutton belts, Beijing, Tianjin, Shanghai and Northwest China's dairy belts, and the Yellow Sea and the Bohai Sea's aquatic belts.

2. Vigorously developing the animal farming industry. We will strengthen and expand animal husbandry, enhancing breed improvement and animal disease prevention and control, and promoting scale, standardized, intensive and modernized livestock and poultry farming. We will promote the healthy and stable development of pig farming and actively support the construction of standardized scale pig feed production bases (farms). We will improve pig farms' rearing conditions, epidemic prevention and manure treatment, and strengthen the construction of the public live pig disease prevention and control system. We will enhance the subsidy system for pig farming and the quality-breed promotion policy, and further strengthen the support for pig production via credit loans and insurance. We will continue to implement the incentive policy for top pig-producing counties (farms). We will accelerate the restructuring of the dairy industry and ensure the quality and safety of dairy products, thus promoting the lasting and sound development of the industry. We will step up promotion of beef and mutton production, stabilize the development of poultry and egg production and encourage the development of special livestock breeding. We will promote the healthy development of the aquatic products industry, expand ecological aquacultural farming, and assist and grow ocean fishing.

3. Accelerating the development of resource-efficient agriculture. We will promote the application of channel seepage prevention, pipeline transport of water, spray irrigation, drip irrigation and other water-conservation agricultural technologies. Efforts will be made to promote high-efficiency water-saving irrigation and to raise the area of farmland covered by water-saving irrigation facilities by 50m *mu* (3.3m hectares). Efforts will also be made to develop rain-fed agriculture. We will speed up the construction of rain-fed agriculture demonstration bases, adopt plastic mulching, rainwater collection for supplemental irrigation, conservation ploughing and other techniques. We will advocate intensive farming, develop intercropping techniques and promote stereoscopic planting, thereby raising land use efficiency. We will raise the efficiency of agricultural inputs by promoting the application of agricultural technologies that economise on the use of seeds, fertilizer, pesticide and energy.

Developing rain-fed agriculture in arid regions

Gansu Province, located in northwest China, has 36m mu (2.4m hectares) of dry land, accounting for 70% of all its arable land. Gansu receives average annual rainfall of 300mm, most of which occurs between July and September. The harsh climate is not favorable for agriculture. In recent years, however, Gansu has produced bumper harvests with record highs.

The high output results from the development of science and technology. Whole-film double-furrow sowing, or two furrows (one wide and one narrow) both covered with plastic mulch, have increased the efficiency of re-using rainwater by retaining it in the soil to water crops. The mulch reduces evaporation; the furrows transform the spring rainfall into available water resources by collecting it in seeding furrows through rainwater harvesting surface to make it possible for seeds to fully absorb the rainfall. By using this method, the efficient use of rainfall has doubled. It is estimated that the normal annual corn yield increases by 35% more than half-film planted corn, and the potato yield grows by 30% more than open field potatoes.

A steady high output relies on planting crops that are suited to the climate. As whole-film double-furrow sowing is becoming popular, Gansu is restructuring its agriculture, increasing the high-yield autumn crops such as corn and potatoes while reducing winter wheat in the arid areas. Statistics show that in 2010 there were about 12.74m mu (850,000 hectares) of corn land, compared with 6.97m mu (465,000 hectares) in 2000; the potato land expanded to almost 10m mu (670,000 hectares) from about 6.26m mu (417,000 hectares); the ratio of summer crops to autumn crops changed to 38:62 from 51:49. Nowadays, corn and potatoes have become a crucial support for Gansu's stable and increasing agricultural output.

"Last year, I harvested 13 tonnes of corn and earned a lot of money. I used cornstalks to feed my cattle, and used their manure to fertilize the land. They've benefited from each other," said Ma Shaoyuan, a 70-year-old farmer in Zhoujiazi Village, Qijia Town, Guanghe County, Gansu Province. Over 10m mu (670,000 hectares) of land has been planted with corn, increasing the total grain output and providing fodder for livestock grazing. Guanghe County, together with several other counties in Gansu, is exploring a circular agriculture model: dry farming – cornstalks – cattle and sheep breeding – biogas-organic fertilizer – grain output increase. In 2010, the proportion of livestock grazing in Gansu increased to 45%, 7% higher than in 2000.

Gansu: the 'hope project' showcasing film technology application on arid plateau

4. Actively develop urban agriculture. Capitalizing on the science and technology, human resources and market space in urban areas, we will strive to deepen and strengthen the development of functional agriculture, including technology-intensive agriculture, facility agriculture, ecological agriculture, quality agriculture and agritourism. To secure 'vegetable baskets' in the suburbs of large and medium-sized cities, China is supporting the construction of farming bases for the production of vegetables and other fresh produce.

Shanghai: A leader of modern urban agriculture

Shanghai is 'far removed' from agriculture due to its limited agricultural resources and low agricultural output as a percentage of its GDP. However, the city has become an agricultural powerhouse for its urban agriculture development model and high average yield.

Although there is not much arable land available here, Shanghai enjoys advanced science and technology, human, finance, information and market resources, which make it a front-runner in modern urban agriculture. Shanghai's agriculture, which is only 0.6% of its GDP, has delivered a stable supply of agricultural products for years, and especially 90% self-sufficiency in leafy greens. Among 50 major cities in China, Shanghai ranks behind 30 cities in the vegetable price index. With a small population working in agriculture, Shanghai boasts the most modern agricultural parks, amazing high-tech agricultural services and agricultural innovation. It has also enhanced agriculture by integrating it with the secondary and tertiary sectors. The average profit per mu (0.0667) is nearly Rmb5,000, much higher than China's average. Over 1.6m mu (over 100,000 hectares) of arable land serves as a natural and seasonal wetland, a green ecological belt around Shanghai. Agritourism here is now thriving and offers recreation and education, which are becoming a more popular choice for weekend plans among people in downtown Shanghai.

In the past 20 years, Shanghai has witnessed different stages of agricultural development, including the rise of modern urban agriculture. It took the earliest step among all large cities in China toward this new type of agriculture.

In the mid-1980s, Shanghai transformed its rural agriculture into suburban agriculture, a fragile and self-reliant industry that could only provide fresh food and primary agricultural products to the urban areas. At the beginning of the 1990s, as the demand for agricultural products in urban areas increased,

> Shanghai set higher aims for agricultural development. In Shanghai's Ninth Five-Year Plan, the government claimed that the goal of developing urban agriculture was to boost ecological balance, tourism, high-tech agriculture demonstration and exports for foreign exchange. Shanghai's urban agriculture then started. In the late 1990s, Shanghai moved toward modern urban agriculture. As the urban and suburban areas were quickly integrated, the counties and rural districts became an important part of Shanghai. The agricultural support system consisting of finance, science and technology has been improved. Modern facilities and technologies such as greenhouses, sprinklers and drip irrigation have been widely applied for agriculture which has attracted many tourists and students.
>
> In 2007, at the Ninth Shanghai Municipal Party Congress, Xi Jinping, then Secretary of the CPC Shanghai Municipal Committee, stated that Shanghai as an international modern metropolis would give priority to efficient ecological agriculture and promote its influence in economy, ecology and services.
>
> In Shanghai's 12th Five-Year Plan for Modern Agriculture, the government declared the goals of developing efficient ecological urban agriculture, promoting its influence in the economy, ecology and services, and ensuring efficient supply and quality of agricultural products. The government's focus was on a multi-functional modern agriculture.
>
> Shanghai is now transforming the traditional production-oriented agriculture into a modern urban agriculture aiming at the same time at the economy, ecology, high-tech demonstration and services. Agriculture as a percentage of Shanghai's GDP will keep decreasing in the future while it is increasingly integrated and efficient.

Source: *Farmers' Daily*, April 23, 2012.

http://www.farmer.com.cn/jjpd/hyyw/201204/t20120423_713100.htm

5. Developing forestry products. Efforts are being made to enhance: the cultivation of high-quality seedlings and precious tree species; the construction of strategic timber reserves for industrial and commercial purposes; the promotion of forest tourism, bamboo industry, flower seedlings and plants, wildlife breeding and utilization industry, and sand industry; the development of woody crops and oil-bearing plants such as tea-oil trees, walnuts and other specialized forest products; and the development of the underwood economy.

6. Ensuring the quality and safety of agricultural products. People who produce and sell agricultural products need to be educated about the importance and their responsibility for quality and safety. To achieve agricultural standardization, we will improve the system of agricultural product quality and safety standards, especially concerning the safety of agricultural inputs, residues of pesticides and veterinary drugs, and the regulation of cultivation practices. A quality tracking system must be established to protect registered trademarks and enforce the geographical indication (GI) protection system. China should promote green, pollution-free, organic food and GI agricultural products. The quality safety inspection system for agricultural products must be strengthened to improve routine monitoring and supervision of the quality and safety of agricultural products. Supervision over the production, acquisition, storage, processing, and sales of agricultural products must also be regulated. Illicit drugs, illegal chemicals and other agricultural inputs that are potentially harmful to human health are prohibited. We will carry out a risk assessment of the quality and safety of agricultural products to improve our risk control capabilities.

III. Accelerate Agricultural Scientific and Technological Innovation and the Widespread Application of Technology

1. Enhancing agricultural technological innovation capability. Based on China's basic national conditions, China should try to establish an agricultural technological innovation system that meets the needs of modern agriculture. To create a better atmosphere for agricultural innovation, we should try to increase the proportion of agricultural projects in the national science and technology program, to set up more innovation funds for agricultural technological development, and to support the construction of national agricultural hi-tech demonstration zones and national agricultural technology parks. Reforms should be carried out for agricultural research institutes, including improving the operation and evaluation mechanisms of scientific research projects, building a business-oriented strategic alliance for agricultural technological innovation, and supporting high-tech enterprises to engage in the research and development of agricultural technologies and in national-level high-tech projects, which would help to establish an advanced mechanism for agricultural innovation. Agricultural education and technology training should also be strengthened to speed up the development of human resources for agricultural technological innovation.

2. Making breakthroughs in critical basic theory and key technologies. China will promote basic research in agriculture, especially in agricultural, biological gene regulation and molecular breeding; in resistance mechanisms for crops, forests, animals and plants; in efficient use of agricultural resources; in ecological rehabilitation of crops and forests; in pest control; and in biosafety and agricultural products safety. Meanwhile, we will speed up the development of cutting-edge technologies and aim to achieve innovative results in agricultural biotechnology, new materials, advanced manufacturing and precision agriculture. Efforts will be made in the innovation, integration and promotion of cost-effective and energy-saving agriculture, water-efficient irrigation, agricultural equipment, new types of fertilizers, animal disease control, processing and storage, circular agriculture, offshore agriculture and rural livelihood. To create an information-based agriculture, we will work on data collection and management, resource research, weather and natural disaster forecasting and early warning systems.

3. Strengthening and consolidating the seed industry. Besides the conventional breeding research, China will increase the investment in basic and public research to enhance the collection, conservation and identification of germplasm resources; to develop innovative breeding theories and technologies; to improve breeding materials; and to generate new genetically modified organisms and high-yield seed varieties. We will modernize the whole seed industry based on production, education and research to acquire the functions of seed cultivation, breeding and marketing. Large competitive seed enterprises will be established through integrating industry resources, optimizing resource allocation, raising market access standards and promoting mergers and acquisitions among seed enterprises. Innovation will be emphasized in biological breeding as well as in improving animal and plant varieties. We will also attach great importance to the construction of high-performance seed breeding bases and new seed variety demonstration zones in counties and towns that play an important role in the production of crops, cotton and oil-bearing plants. Seed market supervision will also be strengthened by improving and completing the validation, protection and withdrawal policies, and upgrading the administrative licensing of seed production and operation.

Li Denghai: father of China's compact hybrid maize

Li Denghai, born in Laizhou City, Shandong Province in September 1949, is known as the 'father of China's compact hybrid maize' and is as renowned as Yuan Longping, the 'father of hybrid rice'.

How to Promote the Modernization of China's Agriculture

In the past 30 years, Li has achieved seven record highs in the yield of summer maize and set a record of 1,402.86kg per mu (21.043t/ha) in 2005 which still stands to this day, allowing each mu to feed 4.5 people, whereas in the past that used to feed only one person. He was the first to develop the compact hybrid maize that includes 52 national and local-level approved varieties. The maize varieties that Li cultivated have been introduced onto nearly 1bn mu (67,000 hectares) of land, achieving a profit of Rmb100bn.

After graduating from middle school in 1972, Li joined the agricultural technology team of his village as the team leader. He was impressed when he discovered that the spring maize produced by DuPont Pioneer had a yield of 1,250kg per mu (18.75t/ha). He was determined to create China's own maize seeds with a higher yield than American maize. In 1974, he was recommended to Laiyang Agricultural College (now Qingdao Agricultural University) for special training. Liu Enxun, the college teacher, gave him 20 valuable hybrid maize seeds named XL80. Yu Yi, an expert in maize cultivation, suggested that he try an upright-leaf maize type that could be thickly planted and with the potential to produce a higher yield than conventional spreading-leaf maize.

In 1979, Li separated a new variety Ye 107 from XL80 and used it as the parent plant to produce 7.2kg of hybrid maize seeds in Hainan. These seeds, known as Yedan 2, produced a record yield of 776.6kg per mu (11.65t/ha). Since then, Li has developed a series of new varieties from Yedan 6 to Yedan 12 with a yield per mu ranging from 824.9kg (12.373t/ha) to 953kg (14.295t/ha) and

> *ultimately to 962 kg (14.45t/ha). In October 1989, Li set a new world record with Yedan 13 that produced 1,096.29kg per mu (16.444t/ha). Therefore in 2004, he won the first prize of the National Science and Technology Progress Award. Some 16 years later, on October 17, 2005, a super maize DH3719 was created with a yield of 1,402.86 kg per mu (21.043t/ha). He had broken the world record again.*
>
> *In his 38-year experience with maize cultivation, Li Denghai has broken China's record of summer maize production 7 times, and broke the world record 2 times. He has led the development of China's compact hybrid maize, hence he came to be called 'father of China's compact hybrid maize'.*

4. Promoting the popularization of agricultural technological capability.
To make agricultural technologies more accessible in rural areas, we will establish county and town-level and regional public service organizations dedicated to agricultural technology promotion, animal and plant disease control and agricultural products quality control. Systems of management, recruitment and evaluation will also be established. China will also raise the pay of workers to promote agricultural technology in rural areas to the salary level of rural public servants; while financial support should be given to build a top-down agricultural technology promotion system in all agricultural counties and to ensure that every county or town is accessible to agricultural tech programs. We should implement a market-based mechanism for the public-oriented functions of the agricultural promotion institutions and explore multiple channels to achieve public support for agricultural development. Cooperation will be enhanced between universities and research institutions on one hand and the agricultural promotion institutions and farmers' professional cooperatives at the grassroots level on the other, as well as between leading agricultural enterprises and individual farmers, to achieve an effective integration between technological innovation and agricultural production and operation. Colleges, universities and research institutions will be encouraged to set up agricultural demonstration bases to facilitate the integration, development and commercialization of agricultural technologies. China aims to establish a well-functioning agricultural technology market by fostering the diversity of competitors, improving regulations for trading and operation, and enhancing agricultural IPR protection.

IV. Improving Agricultural Facilities and Equipment

1. Carrying out more water conservancy projects. China will continue to build infrastructure to support large and major mid-sized irrigation areas and upgrade their water conservancy facilities. New irrigation areas will be established in areas with abundant water and land resources to increase effective irrigation of arable land. To improve the irrigation and drainage system, we will upgrade large and medium-sized irrigation and drainage pumping stations and the transformation of flooded areas. The existing irrigation facilities will be given full play, and for this purpose the major infrastructure to support construction and water conservancy upgrading projects for 70% of irrigation areas and 50% of medium irrigation areas will be completed. The construction of water conservancy projects will be accelerated in key counties and the supporting facilities among irrigation fields will be strengthened. Based on the local geographical environment, one or more choices of five small-scale water conservancy projects will be implemented: small water cellars, small ponds, small reservoirs, small pumping stations, and small canals leading to mountainous and hilly areas. Efforts will also be made to develop water conservancy facilities in pastoral areas with the construction of water-efficient irrigation facilities for forage land.

2. Expanding the construction of high-standard farmland that produces good yields in times of drought or excessive rain. We will speed up the transformation of at least 400m *mu* (27m hectares) of medium and low-yielding farmland into high-standard farmland that produces good yields in times of drought or excessive rain. A system of measures will be taken, with clear focus on key areas and key measures including land leveling, soil improvement, raising soil fertility, building tractor roads and forest planting amid fields according to the corresponding requirements and standards. We will establish and improve mechanisms for the management and protection of farmland and agricultural facilities to ensure the long-term yield benefits. A sound management system for farming facilities will be set up to ensure their long-term functionality.

3. Accelerating agricultural mechanization. Support will be given to upgrading the agricultural machinery industry, especially the research and development of critical components and products to improve their applicability, convenience and safety. Efforts will be made to address the particular challenges in mechanical transplanting of rice and mechanical harvesting of corn, oilseed rape, sugarcane and cotton. We will try to increase the penetration of mechanized production of grain and commercial crops such as cotton, oil-bearing and sugar-bearing plants while increasing mechanization in animal husbandry, forestry, fruit planting and primary processing of agricultural products. We will facilitate the development of agricultural and mechanical facilities for animal husbandry and aquaculture. We will extend the application of mechanical technologies for subsoiling, precise sowing, deep fertilizing, conservation ploughing and recycling of crop waste. By integrating agricultural machinery and processes, we will try to get more farmers to implement mechanized planting. Agro-industry will be encouraged to increase the productivity of fertilizers, pesticides and plastic mulches.

4. Building stronger disaster prevention and reduction capability. We will continue to improve the management and rehabilitation of major rivers, lakes, and medium and small-sized rivers; to consolidate reservoirs with potential risks; to enhance the comprehensive management and conservation of ecologically vulnerable areas; and to increase the capabilities of rivers to withstand floods, mountain torrents and geological disasters. On this basis, we will establish a flood-related disaster prevention and relief system for major rivers by combining engineering and non-engineering measures and to soundly bring under control major, medium and small-sized rivers, including tributaries of major rivers, rivers without tributaries rushing into the sea and inland waterways. We will carry out water source projects to address water shortages due to engineering factors. The meteorological infrastructure and service system will be strengthened to improve agro-meteorological disaster forecasting. To respond more actively to climate change, we will improve: the accuracy and precision of agro-meteorological disaster monitoring and pre-warning systems; the infrastructure of weather modification and research capacity; and the scientific exploitation and utilization of cloud-water resources. To act more efficiently in agricultural emergencies and minimize losses from disasters, we will strengthen disaster monitoring, pre-warning and response coordination. We will secure relief supply reserves, and upgrade emergency reporting and disclosure. We will improve the surveillance and control systems of animal and plant pathogens and their development by carrying out specialized prevention and control methods against forest pests and grassland rodent pests. A sound forage reserve system must be established to increase the capability for disaster prevention and mitigation in pastoral areas. Fishing port construction and fishing boat standardization will be expedited to increase the safety of fishery production.

V. Strengthening the Organization of Agricultural Production and Operation

1. Promote the industrialization of agricultural operations. Policies and measures for agricultural industrialization will be renewed while support in terms of finance, tax and information will be enhanced to build an integrated agricultural system encompassing an extended industrial chain with the functions of production, processing and sales. China will support agricultural leaders with great potential, influence and driving force to engage in technological innovation, production upgrading and brand building. Depending on the leading enterprises, we will establish professional, standard and large-scale production bases and promote the partnership between leading enterprises and farmers' professional cooperatives to organize and motivate farmers.

Jiangsu Province nurtures 'dragon's head' (leading) enterprises to boost new agricultural model

A policy paper was recently released by the general office of Jiangsu Provincial Government to organize a joint conference on agricultural industrialization work, including the provincial agriculture committee, the provincial development and reform commission, the provincial finance department and eight other departments. This was the third official order on boosting agricultural industrialization to foster a new breed of leading enterprises.

In recent years, Jiangsu's agricultural industrialization level has continuously improved and clusters of leading agricultural enterprises have continuously emerged to play an increasingly important role in the agricultural modernization process. According to the provincial agriculture committee, in January 2013 there were 5,447 leading agricultural enterprises at or above provincial level, 470 more than the previous year. The operatonal quality of these leading enterprises registered steady improvement. By the end of 2012, 443 of them had reached a sales turnover of more than Rmb495.5bn (US$80bn), and realized a net profit of Rmb15.257bn (US$2.46bn), representing increases of 25.86% and 10.17% respectively, with 11 of the enterprises achieving a sales turnover of more than Rmb10bn (US$1.611bn), This gave the impetus for 9.53m households to be involved in agricultural industrialization, which was 10.22% up over the previous year, accounting for 1/3 of China's total. In 2012, 443 leading agricultural enterprises at or above the provincial level gave the impetus for 9.53m households.

"Improving the operating performance of leading agricultural enterprises is the key to promoting agricultural industrialization and to boosting a new breed of agricultural business," said Xu Huizhong, Deputy Director of Jiangsu Agriculture Committee. In recent years, Jiangsu has become the first province in the country to organize activities 'to promote a year marking the improvement leading agricultural enterprises' operating performance' to encourage its enterprises to establish a steady purchase-sale chain and raw material production bases via independent operations, partnerships and outsourcing to specialized suppliers, in order to increase farmers' incomes. Meanwhile, Jiangsu issued 'Suggestions on Supporting Leading Enterprises in Agricultural Industrialization', offering official assistance for financial services and enterprise competitiveness.

To support the provincial agricultural leaders and potential leaders, Jiangsu has set up a special fund for provincial agricultural industrialization. In 2012, Jiangsu spent a total of Rmb230m (US$37m) for this purpose, benefiting 240 leading enterprises. It has signed a strategic cooperation agreement with the Jiangsu branch of the Agriculture Bank of China (ABC), committing Rmb132m (US$21.3m) credit in total. The Jiangsu government, the provincial agriculture bank, the Nanjing Yurun Group and four other enterprises pledged a total contribution of Rmb100m (US$16.11m) to establish Jiangsu Huilong Investment Guarantee Corporation to provide financing guarantees for agricultural enterprises. City and county-level competent authorities have implemented five effective measures to promote agricultural industrialization with clear requirements, plans, goals and responsibilities: to establish a local agricultural industrialization base; to make local farmers rich; to revitalize agricultural industry; to cooperate with farmers' cooperative organizations and to create a competent agricultural brand. On the other hand, the leading agricultural enterprises, equipped with technology, market resources and information, have actively engaged themselves in these activities, playing an important role in establishing farmers' professional cooperatives, enhancing partnerships with leading growers and breeders, and farmers' organizations. They have worked to strengthen their competence by building their own brands supported by organic, ecological and original products.

This year, a new challenge has arisen: how to lift agricultural industrialization to a new level? Pan Changsheng, chief of the agriculture industrialization guidance office, has proposed five initiatives: 1. Continue the development of model agricultural leaders to ensure growth of 10% and 8% respectively in annual sales and the number of farmers' households involved; 2. Accelerate the construction of local original industrial base, encouraging local competitive industries to develop in favorable areas to form a multi-functional and coordinated modern agricultural industry system; 3. Support the construction of agicultural processing clusters and attract agricultural leaders to start up businesses there to promote industrial clustering; 4. Make efforts to build a modern circulation system for agricultural products with the aim that 10% of agricultural enterprises should achieve over Rmb10bn (US$1.611bn) in annual sales; 5. Improve administrative services, and support enterprises or bases (parks) to develop their research and development (R&D) capability, product inspection and testing, and information network construction. Besides these measures, the 382 provincial leadeing agricultural enterprises in late 2012 should be monitored on an ongoing basis and only the fittest should be able to keep this title.

Source: *Farmers' Daily*, February 28, 2013

http://www.farmer.com.cn/xwpd/jjsn/201302/t20130228_813663.htm

The development of a leading industrialized agricultural enterprise

In 2003, Chen Shigui, a farmer in Wangjiafan Village, Yidu City, Hubei Province, founded the 'Tulaohan' (Local Old Fogey) Ecological Agriculture Development Company. He bought agricultural sideline products, which were regarded as weeds by most farmers, and processed and packaged them elaborately. Then these products were sold in supermarkets in cities and became very popular. In just a few short years, 'Tulaohan' has developed from a small rural workshop to become an important provincial-level leading enterprise. 'Tulaohan' has created an iconic agricultural brand renowned in Yichang, the province of Hubei and even throughout China.

'Tulaohan' focuses on traditional household foods in rural and mountainous areas, and develops them based on market demand. It insists on strict quality control in each production step, to ensure every product is pollution-free and all natural. Soon after its incorporation, it has developed 14 product categories with 35 varieties.

In April 2006, Chen Shigui's Hubei Tulaohan Ecological Agriculture Development Company merged with Yidu Municipality's Honghuatao (Safflower Set) Town Tangerine Cooperative, another agricultural giant in Yidu, to integrate their resources and advantages. After sufficient negotiation, Chen Shigui agreed to start up Yidu Tangerine Group Cooperative based on Honghuatao Town Tangerine Cooperative and 10 other tangerine cooperatives in Yidu. He implemented standardized production and strict quality control as *well as emphasizing marketing strategy and R&D. With the brand strength of 'Tulaohan', his tangerine business has been expanding further and further.*

Site of Tulaohan Ecological Agriculture Development Company factory

Now the enterprise has already developed three major product categories: 1. Selected Yidu tangerine and deep-processed tangerine products; 2. Seasonings (tangerine-flavored vinegar, soy sauce for cooking fish and black bean sauce); and 3. Snacks (dried fish, dried tangerine peel and preserves). Its products have won accolades such as 'Top 10 Specialties of Three Gorges Region', 'Most Popular Products of Hubei Province' and 'Famous Brand Products of Hubei Province'. They are also one of the best sellers in agricultural markets, branded supermarkets including Walmart and Carrefour, Zhongbai Holdings Group Co Ltd and Wuhan Department Store Group Co Ltd and in more than 20 large and mid-sized cities like Beijing, Shanghai, Wuhan and Yichang. Selected Yidu tangerines have been supplied for four consecutive years to Zhongnanhai in Beijing where the central government is located. The tangerines have also been exported to Russia, Central and Eastern Europe, Hong Kong and other countries and regions. In 2012, the group produced a sales income of Rmb1.5bn (US$240m) and paid a total tax of Rmb78m (US$12.6 m).

The group is located in Yidu Green Product Innovation Park in Honghuatao Town, covering 700 mu (some 47 hectares). It has a 23,350sqm agricultural and sideline products market, 55,000sqm of standard plants, and an 11,000sqm tangerine production center. Now there are more than 2,000 employees, including 105 professional technicians, 186 people with bachelor's degrees, 9 with master's degrees and 2 with doctoral degrees.

2. Developing farmers' cooperatives. China will fully implement *The Law of the PRC on Farmers' Professional Cooperatives* to accelerate the development of farmers' cooperatives and to support their growth with increasing market competitiveness. Innovation is encouraged to develop diversified cooperative forms, especially to establish specialized cooperatives for production and operation. We will extend the areas and functions of cooperative services and support qualified cooperatives to carry out cooperation in credit, land transfer and other fields. The supply and marketing cooperatives will provide more support to farmers' cooperatives. Farmers' cooperatives will be encouraged to set up agricultural product enterprises or to acquire equity in leading agricultural enterprises. Agricultural product associations will also be encouraged in areas with appropriate conditions.

Whether or not farmers' specialized cooperatives can overcome the dilemma faced by rural products of 'small producers in a big market'

Farmers' professional cooperatives have become China's fourth-largest market players after individual businesses, private enterprises and limited liability companies. According to the recently published report on the 'Development of Farmers' Professional Cooperatives in China 2006-2010', the average income of farmers working for cooperatives was 20% higher than non-cooperative farmers. However, farmers' professional cooperatives are still in the initial stage and have to tackle many challenges in building modern agri-businesses that will enable farmers to compete domestically and internationally.

"Farmers like me want to learn e-commerce so we can sell vegetables on the internet simply with the click of a mouse. But the fact is that we have no time until we get home from the fields in the evening. I only have some basic knowledge," said Zhou Zhongchao, a 55-year-old farmer in Dali County, Shaanxi Province. Since 2007, he has had his own vegetable business: the Zhongchao Vegetable Farmers' Cooperative, together with other vegetable growers in the village. All growers here are required to obey a system of rules concerning variety selection, management and sales. Through sustained development, the cooperative now has more than 800 farmer members. "Before the founding of the cooperative, the price of chilies was Rmb10 (US$1.6) per kilo. Thanks to our systematic management, our chilies have won more popularity because of their better quality, and the price has doubled now." Zhou said that the growers in his cooperative could now earn Rmb7,000–8,000 (US$1,130–1,290) per mu.

Zhao Tieqiao, Deputy Chief of the General Branch of Rural Cooperative Economic Operation Management of the Ministry of Agriculture (MOA), said that 'lack of people' and 'lack of money' are two major obstacles holding back the development of farmers' professional cooperatives. Most migrant workers from rural areas are young adults, among whom few have any sense of a market-oriented economy and management capabilities. Therefore MOA will train 190,000 cooperative directors this year and 15,000 more cooperative professionals in the next decade. Meanwhile, the MOA is encouraging young people in rural areas and village officials who are new college graduates to lead and engage in the development of cooperatives.

In terms of financial support, favorable policies have been jointly issued by the MOA with other relevant authorities. One of the policies is that farmer members should not be charged for selling their agricultural products through the cooperative, and should be exempted from value added tax. A system of credit rating, grants and application will be introduced for cooperatives.

Sales represent one of the biggest challenges for future development. According to experts and professionals in agricultural product marketing, the supply chains from farmers to supermarkets and from farmers' cooperatives to college dining halls will be encouraged, while various marketing activities such as exhibitions, trade fairs and agricultural trade fairs will also be encouraged. "Compared with other market players, small cooperatives may not be competitive. Therefore, effective forms of cooperation are needed to lead farmers and cooperatives to participate in market competition on a larger scale and at a higher level. For instance they could compete via specialized and associated cooperatives," said Zhao Tieqiao.

At the same time, cooperatives are encouraged to establish direct-sales stores, chain stores and retail agencies in residential communities and agricultural product markets in cities to realize a seamless transfer of agricultural products from farmers' land to consumers' tables.

In Zhao's view, farmers' professional cooperatives connect agriculture, farmers and rural areas. Supporting policies are needed in the future. Government support, however, serving as the guiding power, cannot decide the development of the cooperatives. It is important for them to build and increase their cohesion by implementing standard and democratic management, and establishing a system of governance including general meetings, council groups, supervisory boards and distribution channels.

How to Promote the Modernization of China's Agriculture

Source: Xinhua News Agency, October 30, 2011

http://news.xinhuanet.com/fortune/2011-10/30/c_111133437.htm

3. Establishing a new non-government agriculture service system. China will accelerate institutional construction based on public service agencies and cooperative economic organizations, with the support of leading enterprises, and non-government participants will be encouraged to be part of this system. This system will combine public service and commercial functions, providing both specialized and comprehensive services. We will nurture and develop a wide range of socialized agricultural service organizations and lead farmers' professional cooperatives, supply and marketing cooperatives, special technology associations, rural water cooperative organizations, agriculture-related enterprises and other non-government participants to provide agricultural services before, during and after production. We will ensure that rural collective organizations will provide better services for farmers' production and operation.

4. Developing a modern agricultural products circulation system. To improve the agricultural products market system, we will build up and upgrade wholesale markets for agricultural products; and speed up the establishment of a wholesale market network with a scientific design, advanced facilities, all-round functions and a well regulated trading environment. We will upgrade trading services, support facilities and the management of agricultural products markets; develop a well regulated trading environment; and reduce operating costs. We will promote an agricultural futures market which will provide orientation for production, stabilize the market and hedge against risks. A modern circulation system for agricultural products will be established via the construction of infrastructure such as large logistics centers, cold chains for agricultural products and distribution centers for fresh agricultural products. Comprehensive pilot programs for modern circulation will be implemented for south-north vegetable transportation and west-east fruit transportation. Efforts will be made to develop the farmer-supermarket supply chain and healthy e-commerce for agricultural products, and ultimately to build up an efficient circulation network. We will foster and train rural brokers, agricultural product marketing specialists, agricultural products circulation enterprises and other market players to create an organized and industrialized circulation system for agricultural products.

Table 2-3: Key indicators of modern agricultural development during the 12th Five-Year Plan period (2011-2015)

Categories	Indicators	2010	2015	Average Annual Growth (%)
Supply of agricultural products	Overall grain production capacity (million tonnes)	>500	>540	
	Grain cultivation area (million hectares)	110	>107	
	Total cotton output (million tonnes)	5.96	>7.00	>3.27
	Total output of oil-bearing crops (million tonnes)	32.30	35.00	1.62
	Total output of sugar crops (billion tonnes)	120.08	>140.00	>3.12
	Total meat output (million tonnes)	79.26	85.00	1.41
	Total egg output (million tonnes)	27.63	29.00	0.97
	Total milk output (million tonnes)	37.48	50.00	5.93
	Total output of aquatic products (million tonnes)	53.73	>60.00	>2.23
	Overall pass rate in routine monitoring program for quality and safety of agricultural products (%)	94.8	>96.0	>[1.2]
Agricultural mix	Animal husbandry share of total agricultural production value (%)	30	36	[6]
	Fisheries share of total agricultural production value (%)	9.3	10	[0.7]
	Agro-processing share of total agricultural production value (%)	1.7	2.2	[0.5]
Agricultural infrastructure	Newly increased farmland with effective irrigation (million hectares)			[2.67]
	Effective utilization coefficient of water for farmland irrigation	0.50	0.53	[0.03]
	Total power of farm machinery (GW)	920	100	1.68
	Comprehensive mechanization level of ploughing, sowing and harvesting (%)	52	60	[8]
Agricultural technology	Contribution of advanced science and technology (%)	52	>55	?[3]
	Rural population with practical skills (million)	8.2	13.0	6.8
Organization of agricultural production and operation	Number of farmers' households benefiting from vertically integrated agriculture (million)	107	130	3.97
	Proportion of large-scale dairy cattle farming (herds of 100 or more) (%)	28	>38	>[10]
	Proportion of large-scale pig farming (units of 500 or more) (%)	35	50	[15]

Agricultural ecological environment	Penetration of appropriate household biogas digesters (%)	33	>50	>[17]
	Comprehensive utilization rate of straw (%)	70.2	>80.0	>[9.8]
Agricultural output value and farmers' incomes	Annual growth rate of added value of crop production, forestry, animal husbandry and fisheries (%)			5
	Agricultural migrant labor force (million)			[40]
	Per capita net income of rural residents (Rmb)	5,919	>8,310	>7

Notes: 1. [ ] indicates cumulative number over five-year period;
2. By the end of 2008, there were 8.2 million rural residents with practical skills;
3. The per capita net income of rural residents is calculated at 2010 prices and the growth rate is calculated at comparable prices.

Source: *National Plan for the Development of Modern Agriculture (2010-2015)* **issued by the State Council on January 13, 2012.**

Chapter 3

How to Carry Out Construction of a New Countryside in China

China is experiencing the largest ever scale of urbanization. It is expected that by 2030 China's population will peak at 1.5bn and that the urbanization rate will reach 70% under the most optimistic estimate. It means that in 20 years, more than 300m people will move into cities and towns from the countryside. This will be an unimaginably tough challenge. Even so, there will still be 400m to 500m farmers living in rural areas. Therefore, urbanization will be promoted in an active and steady manner while a new countryside must be constructed. Both tracks must be pursued in parallel.

In October 2005, the CPC Central Committee's *Proposal for Formulating the 12th Five-Year Plan for China's Economic and Social Development (2011-2015)* was issued at the 5th plenary session of the 11th Central Committee of the CPC. As part of the proposal, the CPC pointed out that a new socialist countryside will be one of China's major historic missions in modernization. Aiming at advanced production, affluent living, civilized rural communities, a clean and tidy village environment and democratic administration, steady progress will be made in building a new socialist countryside in accordance with local conditions, reality and farmers' wishes.

This begs the question: how to build such a new countryside? At the 4th plenary session of the 16th Central Committee of the CPC in 2004, 'two trends' were raised based on an analysis of the development experience of industrialized countries. In the initial stage of industrialization, agriculture serves as a supporting force for the growth of industry (manufacturing) while, when the country has become industrialized, manufacturing begins to 'reciprocate', or boost, agriculture, and cities support rural areas, resulting in balanced development between urban and rural areas. In December 2012 the Central Economic Work Conference asserted that China had entered

How to Promote the Modernization of China's Agriculture

the development stage when manufacturing would boost agriculture and cities drive the development of rural areas. In November 2012 the 18th CPC National Congress report stated that urban and rural integration would be the fundamental solution for solving issues relating to agriculture, farmers and the rural areas. China will further promote urban and rural integration, boost rural development, narrow the gap between urban and rural areas, and promote their common prosperity.

China's industrialization started with heavy industry which was taken as the first step to get rid of economic backwardness right after the founding of the PRC. At that time, the socio-economic development level was very low. In 1952, China's GDP per capita was just over US$50; the agricultural labor force accounted for 83.5% of the total labor force and the net agricultural output was 70% of the country's total. Therefore, agriculture was the major source of income to fund industrialization. It is estimated that in the 29 years leading up to 1979, the agricultural sector had provided Rmb450bn (US$72bn) for industrialization. This policy was necessary and effective overall, but the backward technologies of agricultural production would not have been developed if this long process had lasted any longer. Moreover, the longstanding separation between urban and rural areas hindered the free exchange of production factors. The huge rural labor force was confined to rural areas, and farmers were in fact excluded from China's industrialization. As a result of separate household registration systems, the rights and opportunities were imbalanced and the urban-rural gap was widening. Although the relationship between urban and rural areas has gradually improved since reform and opening up started in 1978, agriculture and the rural areas have remained underprivileged in terms of resource allocation and income distribution as well as development opportunities. The urban-rural separation as a byproduct of a planned economy has remained unchanged. Therefore, the imbalances between agriculture and industry and between urban and rural development have kept the urban-rural gap very wide.

Since the early 21st century, China has made great achievements in industrialization. China's GDP per capita has reached more than US$1,000; the output value of agriculture to non-agriculture is about 15:85; employment in the agricultural and non-agricultural sectors is about 50:50; and the urbanization level has reached 40%. These four indicators show that China has entered the middle stage of industrialization when the non-agricultural industries have taken the place of the agriculture sector as the leading segment in the national economy mix and serve as the driving force for national economic growth. According to international experience, this is the right time to implement a policy for industry to support agriculture. For example, before the Second World War, agriculture provided a strong support to industrial development in Japan. Since the late 1950s and the early 1960s, industry began to fuel the agriculture sector. In the mid-1960s, Korea depended on the agricultural sector to support industry. Since the late 1960s, the tables have turned.

The implementation of a policy for industry to support agriculture depends, on the one hand, on the level of China's industrialization, and on the other hand, on the uniqueness and complexity of China's agriculture and rural areas. Agriculture remains a weak link in the national economy due to its low productivity. More than 60% of China's population live in rural areas where the living standards and the development of education, science and technology, culture and health lag far behind the urban areas. Besides these disparities, the rural areas are faced with tougher challenges to build an affluent society. According to historical experience, farmers' wellbeing determines whether China will have sound development. Only by accelerating the economic development of agriculture and rural areas, especially by increasing farmers' incomes, strengthening grassroots democracy in rural areas, and building a harmonious and healthy countryside to ensure the majority of farmers live a sound life, can China achieve a stable rural society and long-term national stability.

In *Opinions of the CPC Central Committee and the State Council on Promoting the Construction of a New Socialist Countryside* issued in February 2012, together with other official documents, a number of significant measures and solutions were proposed to solve the underlying problems concerning the construction of the new countryside.[1]

The key concept of building a new countryside is to balance urban and rural development and to integrate the separate urban and rural systems by breaking down the institutional barriers. Agricultural development should be considered within the context of the entire national economy, rural advancement should be considered as an important part of national progress, and the increase of farmers' incomes should be given more weight within the distribution and redistribution system of national income while the country formulates plans on development policies, public resources, infrastructure and the industrial mix.

---

[1] See Appendix 1 to Chapter Three: The 11th Five-Year Plan: The Key Project of Building a New Socialist Countryside

The new countryside will be built according to local demand and the wishes of the public, while equal importance will be given to the rural areas both near and remote, and the local features will be highlighted. Efforts must be made to systematically plan counties, towns and villages, while rural infrastructure construction and social development should be balanced to create better and happier living conditions in rural areas.

I. Strengthening the Construction of Rural Infrastructure

By the end of 2005, there were still 50,000 villages without road access in China, half of villages nationwide had no access to tap water (centralized water supply), 300m rural residents had no safe drinking water, more than 60% of rural households had no access to sanitary toilets, and 2% of villages had no electric power supply. Therefore, in building a new countryside, particular importance was attached to building infrastructure.

Since 2006, the central government has substantially increased the investment in rural biogas and provided funding for village development planning and pilot villages. A guiding catalog has been formulated based on local circumstances for village development and environmental rehabilitation, especially for providing access to drinking water, roads, power and fuel. The government has helped farmers to separate residential and livestock living areas. Safe drinking water projects have been accelerated. The construction of the rural road network is being strengthened with the aim of making all towns and villages nationwide accessible by tarmac (cement roads), making all villages in eastern and central China accessible by tarmac (cement) roads, and making all villages in western China accessible by road, and a system of rural road management and protection is being established. Efforts are being made to promote renewable energy, including farmer household biogas, straw-fired biomass power generation, small hydro power stations, solar panels and wind turbines as well as the construction of rural power grids. A universal service fund has been established to enhance the construction of rural data networks, the development of rural post and telecommunications with the aim of making every village accessible by telephone and every town accessible by internet. In accordance with the requirements of land efficiency, complete facilities, environmental protection, energy efficiency and outstanding features, the government is making scientific plans for rural construction, guiding farmers to build their own houses on an appropriate basis and to maintain the original rural landscape.

By the end of 2010, safe drinking water had been made available for 210m rural people; electricity supply with urban standards had been made available to most rural areas; newly built and rebuilt roads reached more than 1.86m km in total; biogas use reached 40m households; and rural housing projects had been successfully promoted.

According to the 12th Five-Year Plan, the central government is committed to building a new countryside which has: safe drinking water, clean energy, convenient transport, comfortable housing and a clean environment. Basic rural infrastructure construction is being strengthened accordingly, as are rural living and production conditions.

1. Improving rural drinking water safety. Great importance must be attached to the water supply and safety in the construction of drinking water facilities including centralized, non-centralized and urbanized water supply systems in rural areas. By 2015, the proportion of rural population with access to centralized water supply will be about 80%. Efforts will also be made to strengthen the operation and management of drinking water projects, to identify people responsible for its management and protection, and to enhance water conservation and quality monitoring to ensure farmers will enjoy long-term benefit from these drinking water projects.

2. Strengthening rural electric power construction. The rural power grid will be upgraded to improve power supply reliability and capacity in rural areas. The equalization of public power services will be accelerated between urban and rural areas with the aim of eliminating gaps in power prices and power supply. To provide nationwide public power services, power facilities will be constructed in areas where people have no access to electric power. On the premise of protecting the ecology and the interests of farmers, small hydro power projects will be carried out with scientific planning and orderly development; counties fully equipped with electric power (electrified, so to speak) will be established; small hydro power facilities will be built to take the place of fuel facilities based on the local conditions; power grids will be built to support rural hydro power facilities.

3. Promoting biogas-focused clean energy in rural areas. To increase biogas penetration in rural areas, household biogas use and development will be promoted, and management and service systems for biogas facilities will be improved. Clean energy will match the rapid development of large-scale animal husbandry. Small and large-scale biogas projects will be pushed forward. Efforts will be made in the research and development of key biogas technologies and efficient use of biogas residue and slurry. To establish a clean, economical and convenient energy system in the rural areas, traditional wood and coal-fired brick beds will be transformed to increase energy efficiency; large straw-based energy projects will be promoted; and newly-built houses will use solar water heating and solar cookers.

4. Enhancing rural road construction. Road construction projects will be continued to make all villages in eastern and central China and 80% of the villages in the western area accessible to tarmac (cement) roads. County and town-level roads will be rebuilt and connected to each other to form a rural road network and increase mobility. Rural and urban transport systems will be integrated to achieve 100% effective reach of buses between villages and towns, and to make 92% of villages accessible by bus. Efforts will be made in bridge and culvert construction, bridge renovation, bus station development and other projects supporting public transportation. Rural road safety, maintenance and management will be enhanced.

5. Enhancing rural housing construction. Local farmers are encouraged to build their own houses through various forms under legal provisions in qualified rural areas. A rural housing security system will be established to renovate more than 8m rundown buildings; to confirm targets and standards of subsidy for housing renovation; to strengthen project quality, safety control, archive management and registration of property rights. Housing shortfalls in state-owned reclamation areas, forest regions and forest farms shall be made up by upgrading shantytowns in the forest regions, and farms and rundown buildings in reclamation areas. The herdsmen settlement project will be continued, which aims to make adequate provisions to settle all herdsmen, including 246,000 homes for nomads. The fishermen settlement project will also be speeded up to provide homes ashore to fishermen who have lived on boats.

6. Continuing the support for rural poverty alleviation and immigrants from reservoir construction regions. According to the *China Poverty Alleviation and Development Program (2011-2020)*, investment will be increased in poverty alleviation and development, especially in large poverty-stricken areas; more support will be provided in old revolutionary base areas, regions inhabited by ethnic groups and border areas; development-oriented poverty alleviation policy will be implemented focused on integrating the development of poverty-stricken areas and the rural minimum living standard security system; subsistence will be made available to the impoverished and measures will be taken to help them get rich as soon as possible. Policies to support the resettlement of immigrants from reservoir building regions will be implemented by increasing financial integration and investment, developing infrastructure and public services in reservoir and resettlement areas, and continuously improving living conditions and developing social facilities in resettlement areas. Pilot projects will be carried out to address the challenges of the poorest immigrants and to give them secure housing and development opportunities.

Wenchuan County, Sichuan: new rural transformation for a new life

Wenchuan County is located in southeast Aba Prefecture in the northwest of Sichuan Province. Breathtaking natural scenic sites in Sichuan, such as Jiuzhaigou Valley, Huanglong Scenic and Historic Interest Area, Mount Siguniang, and prairies are all within easy reach of Wenchuan County. Before it was hit by the earthquake in May 2008, Wenchuan housed 105,436 inhabitants, including 67,438 rural inhabitants and 36,705 people of Qiang minority in 6 towns, 7 villages, and 118 administrative villages within its 4,084sq km administrative area. Acclaimed as the 'hometown of Yu the Great, home of the giant panda, and the place of origin of Qiang ethnic embroidery', Wenchuan is the industrial base of Aba Prefecture and one of the four regions in China in which Qiang people live in tightly-knit communities.

On May 12, 2008, however, a major earthquake struck Wenchuan County, causing catastrophic damage with direct economic losses amounting to Rmb64.3bn (US$9.2bn). Under the firm leadership of the CPC Central Committee and the State Council and the government and party committees of Sichuan Province and Aba Prefecture, the rescue work achieved positive results and the post-disaster reconstruction was carried out smoothly and fruitfully. Economic recovery has been achieved and social stability has been maintained.

Aiming at developing agritourism and rural tourism, during its reconstruction after the earthquake, Wenchuan is committed to developing specialized farming, modern animal husbandry, forestry, and farm products processing, trying to establish a new type of villages and agriculture, which means 'every village has a specialty' and 'every county has a key economic driver'. At the same time, efforts have been made to develop major industries, mobilize major enterprises and establish local brands. Wenchuan aims to build up a modern farming system. Plantations of cherries, kiwi fruit and flowers have been built, which in turn have driven the planting of tea, traditional Chinese medical plants and the development of aquaculture. Efforts have also been made to establish a demonstration area of modern agriculture on the Min River. Within the next five years, unremitting efforts will be made to establish a 50,000 mu (3,333 hectares) kiwi fruit production base with a production capacity of over 10,000 tonnes, a 30,000-mu (2,000 hectares) cherry production base with a production capacity

Wenchuan, rebuilt after the earthquake

of over 10,000 tonnes, a modern animal husbandry base housing about 10m chickens, ducks, pigs, and goats a year, and a flower base along the arid valley area producing about 10m flowers and plants.

By June 2011, in Wenchuan, there were already 20,000 mu (1,333 hectares) of cherry plantations, 30,000 mu (2,000 hectares) of kiwi fruit plantations, 5,000 mu (333 hectares) of flower gardens, 5,000 mu (333 hectares) of tea fields, 15,000 mu (1,000 hectares) of pollution-free vegetable fields, and 40,000 mu (2,667 hectares) of improved hybrid corn fields. Four types of food produced in Wenchuan are certified as green foods; 384 families are raising poultry and livestock on a large scale, each having pens and coops totaling an area of 23.25sq km, earning about Rmb16,000 (US$2,578) annually. There are two newly established bacon processing factories, four large farms, two communities raising poultry and livestock on a large scale, 70 main roads in rural areas stretching 400km, and 112 water projects have been completed to provide drinking water to about 66,500 people in the countryside.

The 12th Five-Year Plan: construction of key rural infrastructure projects

Drinking Water

Safe drinking water will be supplied through centralized and local drinking water distribution systems and by extending urban water pipes to 30m rural residents (including teachers and students in rural schools and people in state-owned farm and forestry stations).

Power Supply

The rural power grids will be renovated and those that cannot meet the increasing electricity demand will be upgraded. Some 1,000 model solar-powered villages will be built, 200 green-energy counties will be established, 300 counties will be electrified with new villages powered by hydro-electricity, and the installed generating capacity of hydropower stations will be increased by 10GW.

Road construction

A total of 1m km of roads will be built or renovated in rural areas, making all administrative villages in eastern and central China and 80% of administrative villages in western China accessible via tarmac or concrete roads.

Biogas Engineering

Household biogas, small biogas projects, large biogas projects and related service systems will be built, making biogas available to more than half of the households in rural areas.

Housing

Some 8m rundown homes in rural areas will be renovated. Accommodation will be provided for employees of state-owned reclamation areas, forest regions and forestry stations. Also 246,000 apartments will be provided for the settlement of nomads and the final aim is for all nomads in China to have a permanent home.

Clean Countryside

Organic waste will be disposed of and recycled properly, while non-organic waste will be collected and transported in a centralized manner. At the same time, rural area afforestation and ground hardening will also be carried out.

Source: China's 12th Five-Year Plan for Rural Economic Development, NDRC, June 2012

II. Accelerating the Development of Social Undertakings in Rural Areas

During the 11th Five-Year Plan period (2006-2010), China strengthened universal compulsory education. No tuition fees are charged for rural students receiving compulsory education, and free books and boarding subsidies are provided for impoverished ones. Compulsory education in rural areas falls into the public finance security system, and a system has been established to ensure that education funds are secure. The central and local governments are all responsible for implementing such a system. The responsibilities of governments at all levels are specified, finance spending on this matter has been expanded, and related procedures have been carried out step by step to better ensure its security. Rural teacher training programs have been carried out, and 50% of teachers in rural areas have attended a professional training program. Related institutions in cities have been encouraged to help farmers by teaching them relevant knowledge, and sending more teachers from cities to teach in rural areas. Distance learning has been introduced in rural primary and middle schools.

We will continue to improve the healthcare infrastructure in rural areas, especially in the township hospitals and clinics, and develop the health service and medical aid systems in villages, townships and counties. Medical workers in rural areas have been trained, and doctors in cities have been encouraged to provide medical services in rural areas. Systems providing medicine and monitoring the sales of medicine have been established. Illnesses such as avian influenza have been guarded against and properly treated. Family planning management and service systems in rural areas have been improved and rural families are taught that 'having fewer children means getting rich faster' and those who comply with family planning are awarded.

We will enhance the setup of cultural centers, libraries and reading rooms in townships and counties. Projects to extend radio and television coverage to every village and to play movies in villages will be carried out. By 2010, all villages with more than 20 families had access to radio and television. Every month, one movie is screened in every village. Fitness programs encouraging farmers to exercise will be conducted. Farmers' lives have been greatly enriched now that there are cinemas, cultural centers and libraries in their neighborhood. Village affairs are publicized and public opinion is solicited in policy-making processes, so that villagers can exercise their rights to be informed, participate, administer and monitor.

We will carry out more training programs to produce more well educated farmers with professional skills and management competence. Technology courses will also be provided to farmers to enhance their skills and knowledge. Professional training will be made available to farmers so that farmers can find other employment opportunities. A host of new farmers who have outstanding farming, craftsmanship, business operation, and technical knowledge will be cultivated through various training programs.

In the 12th Five-Year Plan period (2011-2015), the construction of a new socialist countryside has made remarkable achievements in improving educational standards, making the countryside cleaner, enriching the life of villagers, and providing equal opportunities to farmers in finding jobs, so as to promote social undertakings in rural areas, lift the moral standards of the rural population and achieve comprehensive rural development.

1. Improving education in rural areas. We have allocated more public educational resources to rural areas, border areas, poor areas, ethnic minority areas and revolutionary base areas. Necessary primary schools and the like will be maintained. Facilities in rural schools have been upgraded to improve teaching expertise and accommodate more boarding students, and teachers there are carefully chosen and trained to improve educational results and to realize more balanced educational development across a whole county. Meals contain better nutrition and free books and boarding are provided for rural students receiving compulsory education, and impoverished ones receive boarding subsidies. We will accelerate promotion of universal high school education in rural areas and implement the policy of providing secondary vocational education to rural students free of charge. We will develop pre-school education in rural areas, building more kindergartens so that universal pre-school education can be realized and children can be taken care of in kindergartens. Professional training will be carried out on a large scale in rural areas so that by 2015, we will have produced 13m farmers who excel at farming, business operation and technical knowledge.

2. Improving medical and health systems. We will bring more medical and health resources to the rural areas. Medical and health service systems consisting of county and town-level hospitals and clinics will be improved. In such systems, county hospitals form the core, which will be responsible for disease prevention and control, and health monitoring. Basic centralized medical services will be provided to rural areas free of charge. A rural women's hospital childbirth subsidy will be implemented. Major infectious diseases, chronic diseases, occupational diseases, endemic diseases and mental illness will be brought under control. An emergency system will be built in the rural areas to better cope with health-related crises.

3. Promoting cultural activities and sports. China will adopt related policies and establish agencies to promote the development of cultural activities and sports in rural areas. Cultural infrastructure will be upgraded so as to offer movies, books, papers and plays to rural residents free of charge. More radio and television stations will be built to extend coverage to villages with fewer than 20 families and that have electricity but no television, and to bring satellite TV to rural areas with no broadband access. More village bookstores and bulletin boards will be built and more activities with local characteristics will be carried out. We will promote fitness, exercize and and improve sports facilities.

4. Providing employment services. We will improve employment services in both urban and rural areas, develop a platform where labor in rural areas can get help in finding employment. Services such as advice regarding job hunting and career development, and employment and unemployment registration will be provided to farmers who want to find non-farming jobs. An employment network that is multi-functional, inclusive, and easily available to farmers will be established.

Haidong, Qinghai, offers training programs for job hunters

Haidong district in Qinghai Province, western China, lies to the east of Qinghai Lake. With a population of 1.62m, Haidong covers an area of 13,200sq km, including Ping'an District, Ledu District, Minhe-Hui Ethnic and Tu Ethinic Autonomous County, Hualong-Hui Ethnic Autonomous County, and Xunhua-Salar Ethnic Autonomous County. Its GDP in 2011 reached Rmb21.937bn (US$3.33bn), and the average annual net per capita income of rural residents was Rmb4,599.83 (US$708).

In recent years, governments in Haidong have put employment high on their agenda, and have been committed to promoting training programs to raise the qualifications of the labor force in both urban and rural areas so they can find suitable jobs or start their own businesses.

Professional training projects are conducted to develop talented people. In conducting professional training, which includes programs such as the 'sunshine project' and the *'rainfall project'*, rural laborers have received training so that they can do non-farming jobs, and migrant workers can receive training for employment and business start-ups. About 184,000 rural workers, 79,000 migrant workers, 76,000 laid-off workers, and 3,068 people who want to start their own businesses have taken part in such training programs.

In the past, farmers mainly went from one place to another within the district to find short-term or part-time manual jobs that required a physically strong body. Now, they have been turned into well qualified workers who are fit for long-term jobs where they can make use of their skills. Labor transfer has become well organized and many people have started their own businesses. The aim of making workers mobile and helping them find jobs, settle down, and become well-off is being realized. The economy has been stimulated and poverty has been reduced. Local brands such as 'Hualong Beef Noodle' and 'Xunhua Salar Resturant' have gained an increasing reputation. Over the past years, more and more people have discovered other ways than farming to make a living, and their income has been getting higher as they become more skilled, representing a good momentum for economic growth. In 2012, making beef noodles and picking cotton and wolfberries were major sources of demand for labor, so Haidong government organized migrant workers and sent 61,111 of them to pick cotton in Xinjiang Province and 24,758 to pick wolfberries in Haixi City while providing necessary assistance to them. This employment produced a total income of Rmb420m (US$66.7m).

It is estimated that by the end of the 12th Five-Year Plan period, 60,000 people will have found new jobs and three million jobs will have been created for migrant workers, bringing services income to Rmb5bn (US$800m). The unemployment rate is under 3.5%. In all, 240,000 people will have received professional training, including 40,000 laid-off workers, 160,000 farmers and 15,000 people who want to start their own business.

III. Raising the Rural Social Security Level

In the 11th Five-Year Plan period (2006-2010), China established a pension insurance system in rural areas to align the level of development in rural areas with social security elsewhere. A new rural cooperative healthcare system has been established in the rural areas. A basic living allowance has been allocated to people living below the poverty line in some areas. Social assistance systems have been set up to provide a living allowance, aid relief or assistance in the form of food, clothing, medical care, housing and burial subsidies.

By the end of 2010, social welfare in rural areas had been improved, basic living allowance systems had been set up, 96.3% of rural residents were covered by the new rural cooperative medical care system, pilot programs to explore new pension insurance systems had been carried out in 24% of rural areas, and more than 50m rural residents had been included in a basic living allowance. Poverty alleviation and economic development in poverty-stricken areas have produced obvious effects.

During the 12th Five-Year Plan period (2011-2015), we will further expand social security in rural areas to meet people's basic needs and cover more people while making it more flexible and sustainable so that rural residents can enjoy medical and old-age care and get access to necessary aid in difficult times.

1. Establishing and upgrading the old-age insurance system in rural areas and making sure that every rural resident is covered by such insurance. Farmers' land can only be expropriated after basic living allowances have been provided to them. China will establish new old-age as well as healthcare insurance systems for rural areas and urban areas, and come up with a way to transfer insurance between the insurance systems in urban and rural areas so that both systems can develop at the same pace and eventually be integrated.

2. Perfecting a new type of cooperative health care insurance system. The per capita contribution and fiscal allowance rate will be gradually increased, and the average reimbursement rate and maximum amounts will be increased accordingly. We will improve the medical aid systems in rural areas, scaling up the amount and coverage of aid and grants. We will enhance the connection and integration of the urban and rural medical insurance systems, and encourage areas with appropriate conditions to build up an integrated medical insurance system.

3. Consolidating construction of the social aid system. China will enhance the basic living allowance system, giving all eligible rural senior residents access to assistance in the form of food, clothing, medical care, housing and burial subsidies. These senior residents can choose to stay at home or in a government nursing home. The amount of basic living allowance will be raised in accordance with price trends, and the average annual increase will reach 10%. The system of aid and relief will also be upgraded to provide disabled people in rural areas with more assistance and subsidies to help them live a better life. China will move faster to establish systems to offer help to rural residents in reproduction and child-raising, and provide related assistance to accident victims.

IV. Improving Rural Environment Conservation and Rehabilitation

During the 11th Five-Year Plan period, China made progress in ecological conservation and environmental protection. We have afforested 25.27m hectares of land, raising the forest coverage to 20.36%. Desertification was halted on 230,000 sq km of land. Soil erosion was basically brought under control with 0.817m more sq km of land eroded. A total of 80.17m sq km of grassland that showed symptoms of degeneration, desertification and salinization have been improved. Some 32.4m more sq km of grazing land have been returned to grassland. There are 2,588 nature reserves across the country and 50% of wetlands are under protection. Major progress has been made in ecological rehabilitation of rivers and lakes. Pollution prevention and control, and environment improvement in rural areas are being carried out.

During the 12th Five-Year Plan period, China will make vigorous efforts in developing circular agriculture, promoting clean agriculture and the reuse of agricultural waste. We will promote soil testing so as to determine appropriate fertilizers and encourage farmers to use green fertilizers and to use fertilizers more reasonably. We will promote pest control and recommend the use of biological pesticides and effective, low-toxicity pesticides with low residues. We will recycle agricultural plastic film and packaging, promote the reuse of straw, design farms scientifically, strengthen the prevention and treatment of pollution from animal and poultry farming and aquaculture, monitor soil pollution and treat it effectively to prevent environmental pollution in rural areas.

In places where garbage can be collected and disposed of in a centralized manner, every family will divide their garbage into different categories before dumping it into trash cans, and the village will collect the garbage which will be transported by related township agencies to the county where garbage is disposed of. In other places, garbage will be classified at the point of origin, minimized on the spot and eventually recycled. We will improve the treatment of polluted water in rural areas, and water pollution in big villages or areas near cities will be treated in a centralized way. We will promote the Clean Countryside Project, improving the sanitation and living environment of rural residents. By 2015, 60,000 administrative villages will have completed environmental rehabilitation. Industrial pollution from rural factories will be monitored more rigorously, and urban industrial pollution and other types of pollution will not be spread to rural areas.

Anji: building a new ecological, cultural, beautiful countryside

Anji County is located in northwestern Zhejiang Province 223km from Shanghai and 65km from Hangzhou. The county covers an area of 1,886sq km with a population of 460,000, of which 76% live in rural areas. It consists of 10 towns, 5 villages, 1 subdistrict and 1 provincial economic development zone. Anji is famous for white tea, chair production and bamboo flooring. It was China's first national ecologically advanced county. A number of ecological projects and a pilot program of sustainable development have been carried out, and a national model of beautiful villages and a national model of agritourism and rural tourism have been built there. It is also hailed as one of China's civil counties, clean counties, green counties, and one of Zhejiang's forest counties. It was the first county in China to be granted the 'China Human Habitat Award' and the 'UN Habitat Scroll of Honour Award'. It has been awarded the 'Yangtse Delta Investment Hotspot (Special Prize)' for two consecutive years.

Since 2008, Anji has been implementing the 'Beautiful Countryside Project', trying to make at least 85% of its villages beautiful with the aim of becoming model new socialist villages with a clean environment, affluent life and harmonious communities.

Anji has focused on the following elements: first, beautiful scenery as an advantage to make all villages sightseeing attractions; second, industrial development to modernize villages and improve people's living conditions, which in turn will benefit the conservation of scenery; third, making each village unique; fourth, overall development and planning of the county to make every village and every family part of a bigger transformation plan. In making villages beautiful, every town and village will do its part in accordance with the overall plan while their unique conditions are taken into consideration to meet the goal of development and making ecological improvements.

Anji's GDP in 2011 reached Rmb22.2bn (US$3.4bn). Government revenues amounted to Rmb2.91bn (US$448m) including Rmb1.67bn (US$257m) of local government revenues, ranking ahead of Huzhou City, and at the forefront of Zhejiang Province. The average disposable income of urban residents reached Rmb280,000 (US$43,077), while that of rural residents reached Rmb140,000

Scenic Majianong village in Anji attracts lots of visitors

(US$21,538), which are well above the average of Zhejiang Province. Its environmental conditions are getting better and better as a result of its ecological efforts. Aiming at a better environment, a higher industrialized level, higher civilization and better services, Anji has built a number of infrastructure facilities that benefit local residents, and has made significant progress with a characteristic rural economy, rural professional cooperatives, modern household industry and rural tourism. In addition to its titles as China's bamboo county and ecological county, Anji is starting to be famous for its beautiful villages since carrying out the 'Beautiful Countryside Project' which has brought enormous benefits to its people, and it has become a model for other counties.

Kang Hongliang, the secretary of the CPC's Yutiao Branch, said that Yutiao village has undergone great changes since people started the beautiful village construction. The environment is clean now that everyone knows the importance of good sanitation. In the past, few people would choose remote villages like Yutiao as a travel destination, but now on weekends and holidays, every farmhouse is full of tourists. Beautiful villages have made them rich.

V. Improving Rural Development System Mechanisms

During the 11th Five-Year Plan period, China made breakthroughs with the reform program in rural areas. The agricultural tax has been abolished, investment in agriculture, rural development and the well-being of farmers have been increased significantly, the coverage and size of agricultural subsidies has been expanded, the mechanism for protecting the prices of major agricultural products has been improved, and the policies supporting and protecting agriculture have been upgraded. Reform of collective forest property rights has been advanced, 3.3bn *mu* (220m hectares) of grassland has been contracted to non-government operators, there has been comprehensive reform in rural areas and the reform of the rural financial system has been intensified.

Meanwhile, new steps have been taken to balance urban and rural development. Some institutional barriers separating urban and rural areas have been eliminated. Migrant workers can find better jobs now. In China, there are 242m migrant workers, 153m of whom are working outside their hometowns. Migrant workers have become an important force driving urbanization which is now accelerating. The integration of urban and rural planning, industry layout, infrastructure development, public services, employment and social administration has also accelerated. Rural-urban integration is a clear trend.

However, essential reform goals in rural areas have not been completely realized and the systemic separation between rural and urban areas still exists. Certain policies are still obstructing the balanced distribution of resources between rural and urban areas. So, during the 12th Five-Year Plan period, China will make unremitting efforts to carry out reforms in the rural areas and adopt innovative policies so as to sustain and upgrade the current operational systems in the countryside, let the market play a basic role in distributing resources and strengthen the macroscopic readjustment and control of rural development. An economic system will be built up in the rural areas that meets the demand of the socialist market economy to revitalize the rural economy.

1. Establishing a mechanism to ensure investment in agriculture, rural areas and farmers continues to increase. The central government has stipulated that the increase of investment in agriculture will surpass the rate of increase in regular government revenues. The government's budget for infrastructure investment will prioritize agricultural and rural infrastructure development. The revenues from land leasing will be used for the development of agricultural land and the construction of infrastructure in rural areas. The increase of investment in agricultural technology will also surpass the increase of regular government revenues, so the agricultural R&D investment as a percentage of added value from agriculture will increase. From 2003 to 2012, the central government invested more than Rmb6 trillion (US$1 trillion) in agriculture, rural areas and farmers, which played a big role in boosting agriculture, rural areas and farmers during the golden period of development. The central government's investment in agriculture, rural areas, and farmers has increased from Rmb214.4bn (US$35bn) in 2003, accounting for 13.7% of fiscal expenditure, to Rmb1.228 trillion (US$190bn) in 2012, accounting for 19.2% of fiscal expenditure, representing an annual increase of 21%, 4.5 percentage points higher than the increase of regular fiscal expenditure.

Figure 3-1: Central Government expenditure on agriculture, rural areas and farmers from 2005 to 2012 (Rmb x billion)

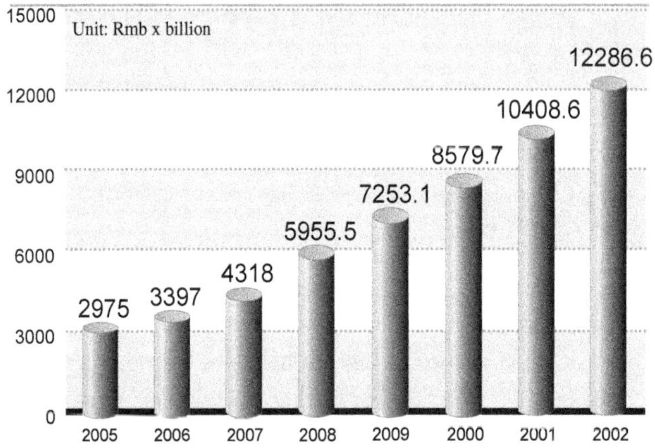

[Bar chart showing:
- 2005: 2975
- 2006: 3397
- 2007: 4318
- 2008: 5955.5
- 2009: 7253.1
- 2000: 8579.7
- 2001: 10408.6
- 2002: 12286.6
Unit: Rmb x billion]

Source: People's Daily, January 22, 2013

(Unit: Rmb x billion

Vertical axis figures: 300, 600, 1,200, 1,500

Graph figures: 297.5, 339.7, 431.8, 595.55, 725.31, 857.97, 1,040.86, 1,228.66)

We will strictly implement the policy that the extra revenue gained from increased taxes on land use will be used solely for agricultural development. We will comply with relevant policy on accounting, withdrawal and use of land leasing income for the development of agricultural land and the construction of irrigation and water conservancy facilities. We will strictly implement the policy that the land use fee of increased building sites will be used solely for the development of farmland and land consolidation. We will try to expand the investment in agriculture by encouraging and guiding private investment in agriculture and rural areas.

2. Continuing and improving the basic rural operation system. We will continue the dual system in which the household contract responsibility system will be the foundation and unified operation coexists with individual operation. We will improve the legal and policy framework for rural land contracts, advance reform of the collective forest ownership system, improve the system of grassland contracts, and improve the household contract responsibility system covering farmland, forest and grassland. We will maintain the current land contracts, make sure that farmers have contracts and certificates in their hands, and that farmers have full operating rights over contracted farmland. We will make sure that farmers have the right to use and benefit from contracted land. We will improve the market for transferring contracted land on the basis of voluntary participation and better service, allowing farmers to subcontract, rent out, exchange, transfer or form partnerships on contracted land to form appropriate scale operations. We will support the development of farmers' professional cooperatives and leading agricultural enterprises. We will strengthen the system of social services and make farmers' operations more organized.

3. Improving farmland management reform. We will promote the confirmation, registration and certificate issuance concerning the ownership of collective rural land, the use right of house-building sites and the use right of collective construction sites. We will improve the administration system for the use of rural house-building land, strictly forbidding the excessive use of land for house building. We will make good use of the current plots of house-building land on the basis that farmers' rights are protected. We will establish mechanisms for compensating farmers once they give up their extra house-building plots. The extra house-building plots and other extra land will be reconverted to farmland and those being turned into collective construction land will be developed in accordance with the overall plan and be subject to the annual construction land quota. Moreover, the need for collective construction will be met in the first place. Pilot projects linking urban and rural construction land will be better regulated and strictly controlled regarding their coverage and size, and the added value of land used for collective construction will be invested in the development of rural areas.

We will establish a unified market for urban and rural construction land plots. We will reform policies on land expropriation, non-profit construction and for-profit construction will be strictly defined and separated, the scope of land expropriation will be reduced, land expropriation will be conducted in compliance with legal procedures, and the compensation system for land expropriation will be improved to increase the amount of compensation under a unified pricing system and make sure the compensation is delivered quickly and in the full amount to village collectives and individual farmers. If, other than planned urban construction, there are for-profit construction projects using collective rural land with approval, farmers will be allowed to participate in the operation of such projects in various legal ways and their legal rights will be protected. The use right of rural collective land for for-profit construction projects will be transferred in the unified urban market of state-owned land. Collective land that is legally obtained for for-profit construction in rural areas will be transferred through the unified land market in an open way and enjoy the same status as state-owned land provided that the land use is compliant with planning.

4. Renovating financial systems to assist rural development. We will stipulate more financial policies in favor of rural development. We will come up with more financing tools and accelerate the combined use of commercial financing, cooperative financing and policy-based financing. We will establish a safe adequately funded rural finance system and provide a multitude of good services. Savings in rural areas will be guided toward investment in the development of agriculture and the rural areas. Loans will be given mainly to local borrowers and the Agricultural Development Bank of China and Postal Savings Bank of China will expand their agriculture-related business. These banks will provide services to farmers, agriculture and rural areas, and their scope of services will be stabilized and expanded. We will deepen the reform of Rural Credit Cooperatives, making full use of their role as the main service providers for farmers, agriculture and rural areas. We will ease access for rural finance service providers, and encourage financial institutions to provide services to rural areas. We will accelerate the establishment of township banks, loan companies, and rural mutual cooperatives, and encourage the establishment of community banks at the county level in certain areas. We will develop small-loan institutions in rural areas. We will strengthen the credit system in rural areas, and allow more warrants. We will develop insurance systems in rural areas and improve related regulations. We will support eligible enterprises with business in rural areas and related fields to go public.

5. Deepening comprehensive reform of the rural areas. We will press ahead with reform of the collective forest ownership system and the stated-owned forest ownership system, and improve the grassland contract system. We will draw experience from pilot projects for comprehensive reforms in both rural and urban areas, and actively explore new ways for addressing issues regarding agriculture, rural areas and farmers.

6. Institutional innovation to promote urbanization development. We will intensify reform of the household registration system, and gradually give citizenship status to migrant workers and their families who have been working and staying in urban areas for a long time. We will relax the restrictions on obtaining urban resident status in small and medium-sized cities to gradually meet the needs of rural residents to settle in urban areas. We will continue to experiment with the establishment of a unified urban-rural household registration system. We will provide better services to migrant workers who don't meet the requirements for obtaining citizenship, making sure that public services are provided to all residents instead of just to registered citizens there. We will make sure that the children of migrant workers have equal access to compulsory education, and come up with a way for them to further their education. We will include migrant workers that have stable employment into the system of basic old-age insurance and medical insurance. We will expand the coverage of work-related injury insurance, unemployment insurance and maternity insurance particularly to include migrant workers and workers in private institutions. We will improve the housing conditions of migrant workers through various ways and encourage various possible means for eligible migrant workers to be included in urban housing insurance. We will take effective measures to solve issues involving second-generation migrant workers. We will push forward pilot projects giving greater autonomy to county governments, increasing the proportion of county-level finance schemes in regional (provincial) finance distribution. In certain areas, county governments may be directly supervised by provincial governments. We will give more rights to fast developing towns with large populations administrative rights to approve investment, business administration and social security.

Appendix I: The 11ᵗʰ Five-Year Plan; key projects in building a new socialist countryside:

The 11ᵗʰ Five-Year Plan (2006-2010): Key projects in building a new scialist countryside

Building grain, cotton and oil production bases and promoting high-quality food industry. *We will establish several large production bases in major grain-producing areas to continuously produce large amounts of good quality commodity grain. We will also continue to build cotton and oil production bases. We will build 10,000 mu (666.7 hectares) of standard farmland in the 13 major grain-producing areas and 484 main grain-producing counties, cultivating improved varieties, strengthening pest control and using advanced agricultural machinery.*

Fertile farmland. *We will make greater efforts to improve the quality of middle and low-yield farmland. We will establish model bases that use upgraded and innovative fertilizing technologies to increase yield.*

Vegetation protection. *We will establish county centers and provincial sub-centers of vegetation protection. We will set up several model bases that excel in preventing disasters, pesticide safety evaluation centers and regional centers for evaluating biotechnology.*

Upgrading facilities to support large irrigation areas and drainage pumping stations in Hunan, Hubei, Jiangxi and Anhui Provinces. *We will continue to build the supporting facilities in large irrigation areas and make them more water efficient. We will renovate and upgrade the drainage pumping stations in Hunan, Hubei, Jiangxi and Anhui Provinces.*

Planting and raising improved varieties. *We will establish a pool of crop varieties, crop variety transformation centers, new variety development bases, seed multiplication farms for livestock, poultry and aquatic products, aquatic breeding centers, and pools and centers of other products.*

Animal epidemic prevention. *We will establish systems for monitoring and early warning of epidemics, prevention and control, quarantine inspection, veterinary drugs quality and residue monitoring, technology support and material supply.*

Farm product quality evaluation system. *We will develop a national farm product quality standard and establish a testing and R&D center. We will establish regional, province-level and county-level farm products quality inspection centers.*

Safe drinking water. *The existing problem whereby there are 100m rural residents drinking unsafe water that has excessive fluorine, arsenic or microbes, or that tastes bitter, or is polluted, and the problem that some areas are suffering from severe lack of water will be solved.*

New roads. *We will build and renovate 1.2m km of roads in rural areas with the aim of making all towns and administrative villages accessible by main roads.*

Biogas in rural areas. *We will transform the livestock pens, toilets and kitchens of rural households and build up biogas projects and biogas tanks. We will establish medium and large-scale biogas projects in some large-scale farms or communities.*

Electricity supply and green energy. *We will build 50 green-energy counties and make electricity generated by wind turbines, solar panels, small hydropower stations, or transferred via extending electricity networks, available to about 3.5m households and meet their demand for electric power supply.*

Rural medical service system. *We will build more county hospitals, maternity and child care institutions, county-level traditional Chinese medicine hospitals (or traditional ethnic hospitals), and especially more township clinics in central and western China.*

Family planning system in rural areas. *We will establish county-level family planning service centers, township family planning service centers and mobile service stations, especially in counties and towns in central and western China.*

Transfer of surplus rural labor to other industries. *We will provide more training programs and employment services to migrant workers and safeguard their legal rights. Migrant workers will have access to legal and policy inquiry services free of charge, job information, job advice and recommendations.*

Chapter 4

How To Increase Chinese Farmers' Incomes and Make Them Rich

Ever since China introduced its policy of reform and opening up in 1978, Chinese rural residents have been enjoying a remarkable increase in income. From 2006 to 2010, their average annual income increased rapidly from less than Rmb3,000 (US$485) a year to Rmb5,919 (US$950), representing an average annual increase of 8.9% (adjusted for inflation) and the fastest growth since 1978. Their living standard has been improved too, spending on consumer durables has been growing exponentially and the consumption structure has upgraded. They also have better food, clothing, housing and transportation. Most impoverished people are sufficiently fed and clothed. However, the gap between the income of urban and rural residents has not been narrowed. In 2009, the absolute income disparity between urban and rural residents was Rmb12,000 (US$1,940); and the relative disparity rate has been expanded to 3.33 to 1. From 2010 to 2012, the income growth of rural residents has been growing faster than that of urban residents for three years in a row, by 10.9%, 11.4% and 10.7% respectively. And the income growth in the central and western regions is higher than that of the eastern region. The gap between the income of urban and rural residents has started to narrow since then. In 2012, the average annual net income of rural residents was Rmb7,917 (US$1,278).

In 2012, at the 18th National Party Congress, the goal was raised for GDP and the average income of both urban and rural areas to double by 2020 compared with 2010. In order to raise the income of Chinese people, the hard part is to raise the income of rural residents. Although, in recent years, rural residents' income has been rising rapidly for nine consecutive years, the growth is still lower than that of the national GDP and that of urban residents' income in the same period. Although in the last three years, the gap between the income of urban and rural residents has been narrowing, the gap is still wide. Besides, the standards and scope in accounting for the income of urban and rural residents are inconsistent. In terms of disposable income, the gap would be even wider. Even if the goal of doubling the income of Chinese people by 2020 is realized, the wide income gap would still exist. So in the future, the rural residents' income will have to grow at par with or even higher than that of urban residents in order to narrow the income gap.

To realize this goal, China will adopt proper policies to adjust the distribution system to put farmers in a favorable position in primary distribution and redistribution of wealth. We will also make sure that the price of farm products rises steadily and that the salaries of migrant workers are on the rise, too. We will increase agricultural investment and farmers' subsidies. We will find ways to help rural residents increase their incomes, in particular from non-farming jobs. We will improve economic development at the county level, and encourage rural residents to find jobs or start businesses outside their hometowns. We will also encourage migrant workers to go back to their hometowns where they can start a business. We will make great efforts to advance the property rights system reform in rural areas, safeguarding the rights of rural residents to benefit from collective resources and revenues.

I. Optimizing the Potential to Increase Rural Incomes

1. Raising the economic effects of agriculture through industrialization, guiding farmers to plant and breed scientifically, and developing high-quality and unique varieties.

Agricultural industrialization is a realistic path connecting 'small production' with 'big markets.' In many countries, there are fully-fledged agricultural cooperatives that provide various services to farmers before, during, and after the production of farm products. For example, in Japan, 90% of farmers are members of Japanese agricultural cooperatives. However, in China, such cooperatives are few. In developed countries, 90% of farm products are processed. In China, the percentage is only 30%. There are few large-scale industrialized agricultural companies, and there is no strong partnership between farmers and enterprises.

Therefore, we will strive to establish a complete industrialized agricultural system, covering all links in the production chain, in which cooperatives produce, process and sell farm products through big industrialized agricultural companies. Farmers can form contract-based partnerships with enterprises directly, or the collectives could buy, process and sell the products while farmers benefit from the revenues, so that the farmers could enjoy the added value from the processing and circulation of farm products.

> ***Farmers' professional cooperatives can break through the difficult situation of 'small producers and big markets'***
>
> *In 2007, Zhou Zhongchao, a farmer in Dali County, Shaanxi Province, set up a farmers' professional cooperative with other vegetable-growers in his village, and he named it after himself: 'Zhongchao Vegetable Cooperative'.*
>
> *"There are many people in our village who plant onions, carrots, garlic, peppers and so on. But different people plant different varieties, and sell the plants on their own, making little revenue," Zhou said. For years, the failure in selling vegetables has gradually made people realize that the only way out is through cooperative production. For the last few years, those who joined the cooperative planted the same vegetables and sold these vegetables together. Now that is already a large-scale business. And more than 800 people have joined this cooperative.*
>
> *Zhou said: "When there was no cooperative, 1kg of peppers could only sell for Rmb20 but now, since there is unified management, the peppers are branded and their quality is good, 1kg of peppers can generate Rmb40." Now farmers who join the cooperative can earn Rmb7,000 to Rmb8,000 per mu (0.067 hectare) of farmland.*
>
> *In the past, every family worked on their own land so the quality and quantity of farm products varied. Now the production is organized through cooperatives, and the producing activities are adjusted in accordance with changes in the market. So the production could be increased to scale operation, and a standard is followed. At the same time, cooperatives can provide funds to farmers and supervise farmers, so the quality of farm products is guaranteed, and products gain credibility which brings more sales.*
>
> *Experts believe that cooperatives can help famers gain more say in the market and extend the industrial chain. Relying more on market demand to decide what to produce, cooperatives can help farmers avoid producing blindly. Cooperatives can also help farmers form partnerships with supermarkets and schools, lowering the transportation cost and increasing farmers' incomes. According to the 'Report on the Development of China's Farmers' Professional Cooperatives 2006-2010', now farmers that join collectives earn 20% more than those who don't.*

Source: http://news.xinhuanet.com/fortune/2011-10/30/c_111133437_3.htm

2. Diversifying agricultural business models, developing tourism, such as farm-stays, agritourism and handicrafts production, and utilizing beautiful scenery and unique customs in the countryside.

Chengdu develops agritourism to create 'Five Gold Flowers'

'Five Gold Flowers', an agritourism recreation area in Jinjiang District, Chengdu City, Sichuan Province, has become a model of agritourism. 'Five Gold Flowers', a 4-star tourist attraction, referring to five recreational farm stays named 'Flower Village', 'Forest of Plum Blossom', 'Jiang's Vegetable Garden', 'Chrysanthemum Village' and 'Moonlight Over the Lotus Pond', is located on the outskirts of Chengdu and includes six administrative villages: Hongsha, Xingfu, Wanfu, Fuma, Jiangjiayan and Da'anqiao, covering an area of 12sq km.

The reason why 'Five Gold Flowers' has developed so rapidly is because it forms a larg-scale coalition, avoiding the risks an individual farmer would face in the market. The five farm-stays have differentiated tourist attractions. Flower Village positions itself as an industrial base of flowers and holds various flower festivals to attract tourists. Moonlight Over the Lotus Pond has 1,074 mu (71.6 hectares) of water and the scenery here focuses on water, lotuses and frogs. Chrysanthemum Village, located in the hills, invites tourists to plant, enjoy chrysanthemum and eat related cuisine to ease their minds and spirits. Forest of Plum Blossom has 200,000 plum trees and attracts tourists to enjoy the beautiful plum blossom and learn more about plums in the plum blossom museum there. And Jiang's Vegetable Garden divides 500 mu (33.3 hectares) of farmland into small plots (0.1 mu each) and rents them to urban residents at Rmb800 (US$133) a year who want to plant things themselves or teach their children about agriculture but don't have the land.

Located at the buffer zone between urban and rural areas, the 'Five Gold Flowers' take advantage of tourism resources in the countryside and combine natural scenery with festivals, recreation, and cultural resources such as ancient towns, forming an agritourism zone that features farm stays, countryside hotels, national model agritourism spots, and ancient towns. It adds lustre to tourism in Chengdu City, shows there is a huge potential for agritourism and promotes the sustainable development of agritourism. The environment, folk customs and the ways of making a living in the countryside have seen changes. Agriculture is going along a path of large scale and industrialized development. The revenue from farmland has increased remarkably. The annual income from growing grain was about Rmb200 to Rmb300 (US$33 to US$50) per mu (0.067 hectares), and the income from growing vegetables or flowers was Rmb2,000 to Rmb5,000 (US$333 to US$833) per mu, but now that figure has increased to more than Rmb10,000 (US$ 1,667).

By developing tourism, more than 3,000 households (more than 11,500 people) are doing tourism-related jobs and have been registered as urban residents, and at the same time help 9,790 farmers to find non-farming jobs. This is conducive to advancing urban and rural integration, contributing to the development of commerce and services in this area. 'Five Gold Flowers' has generated nearly Rmb10m, giving a strong push to the economic development of this area.

New look of Hongsha Village of Sansheng Town, Jinjiang District, Chengdu City, Sichuan Province

3. Adjusting the agricultural structure, utilizing comparative advantages, encouraging 'one product per village', so as to build a number of villages and towns with distinctive features.

Shaanxi Province: 'One product per village' helps raise farmers' incomes

In April 2004, government leaders of Shaanxi Province signed contracts for economic cooperation and exchange with their Japanese counterpart Morihiko Hiramatsu from Oita City, introducing the concept of 'one product per village' to

Shaanxi. *After a variety of investigations and research, the provincial government issued 'The Shaanxi Provincial Program To Establish Thousands More 'One Product Per Village' Model Villages'. Several years later, this movement has already made headway.*

First, an industrial base has begun to take shape. By the end of 2010, 3,823 villages in Shaanxi Province had become 'one product per village' models, 186 villages had become 'one industry per village' models, and 20 provincial-level model villages featuring recreational attractions had been established. About 1.8m rural households and 5m people were involved in major agricultural undertakings, including growing grain, fruit or vegetables, raising livestock, handicrafts, processing farm products, and developing agritourism. About 6,250 farmers' professional cooperatives had been set up; 551 villages had become models in building effective partnerships with big enterprises; and 165 villages had a wholesale market.

Second, production clusters or belts have formed. Based on the advantages of different areas, scientific planning and more investment have been made in 11 counties to set up different industry belts or product clusters, including Luochuan (apples), Zhenping (pigs), Jingyang (vegetables), Shiquan (silkworms) and Wugong (handicrafts). Eighteen counties are accelerating the establishment of five product belts including kiwi fruit, melons, vegetables, tea, konjac (also known as devil's tongue or elephant yam) and Sichuan peppers. The 'one product per village' campaign is linking up different producing areas that complement each other to form synergistic belts and zones. The 'one product per village' model is transforming into 'multiple villages one product', 'one industry per township' and 'one industry per county'.

Third, more brands have been launched. Among the 'one product per village' model villages, 7.5% (288 villages) have developed brands recognized at or above provincial (municipal) level, 3.9% (148 villages) have obtained 'Products with Geographic Symbol of Origin Protection', 6.3% (239 villages) have products with registered trademarks, and 13.3% (471 villages) have pollution-free agricultural products, green food or organic farm products. Special local products are renowned around the world, such as apples from Luochuan, kiwi fruit from Zhouzhi, Sichuan peppers from Hancheng, red dates from Qingjian, green tea from southern Shaanxi, beef from Qinchuan, and clay sculptures from Fengxiang. Those products have become drivers of the local economy and increased people's incomes.

Fourth, many villages have become 'one product per village' model villages.

> *Yusheng Village in Zhouzhi County is a model of developing leading enterprises, Di'erpo Village in Meixian County is a model of service driving production, Huama Village in Jingyang County is a model of production driven by professional markets, Huangying Village in Dali County is a model of stimulating production via leading farmers, Longtou Village in Pingli County is a model of advancing the economy through local specialties, Yuanjia Village in Liquan County is a model of exploiting local customs, and the list goes on. Such models have driven the local rural economy and encouraged other farmers to find more ways to become rich.*
>
> *Fifth, farmers' incomes have increased markedly. In 2010, the average net annual income of residents of 'one product per village' model villages was Rmb5,800 (US$853), an increase of 97.3% from Rmb2,860 in 2006 representing an annual increase of 18.5%, and was 41.3% higher than the average for the whole province, which was Rmb4,105 (US$604). More than 70% of their income comes from leading industries or products.*

Source: Shaanxi: 'One product per village' stimulates agricultural development', February 15, 2013. http://gb.cri.cn/27824/2011/10/27/4985s3416208.htm

II. Actively Develop Secondary and Tertiary Industries in Agriculture

In 2003, among 490m rural workers, 135m transferred from rural areas to work for TVEs. However, in the foreseeable future, despite the fact that an increasing number of rural workers will enter cities, the problem of surplus labor and underemployment in rural areas will remain. Therefore, we must expand their employment in an all-round way. Job opportunities can be created in rural areas by developing secondary and tertiary industries.

1. Strenuously develop the agricultural product processing industry. China will accelerate the development of preliminary processing of agricultural products by improving facilities, thus reducing post-harvest losses and upgrading the market competitiveness of products. Following market orientation, China will try to improve intensive processing of agricultural products, develop processed products based on grain and oil, sugar, fruit, vegetables, meat, aquatic products, dairy products and the processing of characteristic agricultural resources, and turn out safe and nutritious products with high-added value and high quality. Optimize the arrangements of the agricultural product processing industry by encouraging enterprises to consolidate in advantageous regions. Agricultural product processing enterprises will be supported to undergo technological transformation, improve facilities and upgrade technologies, thus enhancing the product quality and creating famous-brand products with high market share.

2. Promote the development level of TVEs. We will urge TVEs to upgrade themselves, step up technological innovation, promote industrial restructuring, improve operating and managing mechanisms, and enhance employee competence and enterprises' core competitiveness. We will promote rural enterprises to conserve energy and reduce emissions, carry out cleaner production and develop a circular economy. We will encourage rural enterprises to establish conglomerates through mergers and acquisitions across regions and industries. Rural enterprises will be centralized or clustered in counties, small towns and parks to increase the clustering effect. We will adopt preferential fiscal policies and provide financial support to enterprises in terms of guarantees, loans and public offerings, thus creating a good environment for the development of rural enterprises. Township and village enterprises will be supported to participate in the development of modern agriculture, the construction of rural and agricultural infrastructure and the supply of public services.

3. Speed up the development of tertiary industries in rural areas. Producer services including finance, information and technology will be developed to meet the demand of rural economic development. We will support cooperative organizations such as commercial and trading cooperatives and farmers' professional cooperatives to develop chain operations and promote rural finance credit marketing. We will firmly implement the '10,000 villages and 1,000 townships' market program to encourage large trading enterprises to extend their services to rural areas, promote the construction of e-commerce systems in rural areas, and to improve logistical systems to increase logistics efficiency. In order to satisfy the needs of rural residents, we will develop consumer services including communication, culture, catering, tourism and entertainment, enrich the variety of service products, enlarge the supply of services and improve service quality. We will also develop services for the aged and community services to adapt to life-style changes brought about by the aging of the population.

New ways for farmers to start local businesses: a survey of e-commerce development in Shaji Town, Suining County, Jiangsu Province

As a symbolic marketing tool in the information age, e-commerce, without any geographical restrictions, is able to offer farmers opportunities to start local businesses because of its low trading costs, simple trading procedures, and unlimited market space. Farmers in Shaji Town, Suining County, Jiangsu Province, have extended their business nationwide and even to foreign countries like Singapore. Nongfeng Village in this town was given 'The Honor of Distinction for Starting E-commerce Business in China's Rural Areas' by the 13th International E-Commerce Conference and Shaji Town was heralded as 'the best place for e-business people' by the organizing committee of the E-Business People's Conference in 2010.

1) Main Methods of Doing Things

1. Supplying direction for the development of rural areas and promoting endogenous development. Because farmers are pragmatic and reluctant to try new things, e-commerce, the new mode of trading and production, needs to be promoted by able people (leaders) in rural areas.

In 2006, the 'three musketeers' Sun Han, Xia Kai and Chen Lei in Dongfeng village started their internet business. At first, they sold pendants and home accessories and later they turned to panel furniture. In order to increase the profitability, Sun Han first invested Rmb100,000 (US$16,110) to build a furniture workshop, using an integrated sales and production model. Their success motivated many rural residents to follow in their footsteps, including the aged, women, the disabled, farmers working away from home, and even middle-level managers of large enterprises. Hu Cuiying was a housewife and her husband and son worked away from home all year round. After noticing that internet commerce was profitable, she asked her family to return home. Later, their family workshop was started, with her son making designs and her daughter-in-law in charge of sales. Liu Xingli, a line manager from Xuzhou Dadi Group, went back home with his wife and set up Sanshi Furniture Company. The influence of the 'three musketeers' spread quickly throughout Dongfeng Village, and even extended to Shaji Town. Now the nearby towns of Lingcheng and Gaozuo, and even Gengche Town in Suqian and Shantou Town in Sichuan Province, have all been affected.

2. Consolidating and upgrading industries. E-commerce has boosted the expansion of furniture production and supporting industries and also the development of industry chains. The supporting industries such as panel processing, furniture accessories and logistics are developing very fast and the industrial chains are being extended. Up until now, there are being more than 200 furniture production plants, one professional service provider for e-commerce, two furniture accessory stores, six panel processing factories and 16 logistics enterprises. With the

expansion of industries, industrial upgrading is a natural next step. At present, the furniture industry in Shaji Town is undergoing a big transformation. Family workshops are being replaced by modern companies, and low-end furniture is being replaced by high-end furniture. Instead of making the same products or imitating others, they offer customized services and make innovations. Besides, they develop their own brands and no longer imitate famous brand products. For example, in 2010, Shaji Town applied for 50 registered trademarks and more than 100 products are trademark-protected.

3. *Self-regulating the industry and standardizing its development.* In order to regulate the industry, promote its healthy development and gain a greater say in the material supply chain, the telecommunication network and logistics, Shaji Town has established an e-traders' association. Through experience sharing, joint purchasing and business training, the association has attracted a lot of members, set up rules applicable to all members and regulated the e-traders' management. Sun Han, the president of the association, said, "We have over 200 members. Through consultation, a system of rules and regulations have been established. Now we are formulating technical standards for furniture quality in Shaji Town and e-commerce customer service standards to better regulate the industry's production and services."

4. *Services follow-up backed up by management.* The development boom in newly emerging industries cannot be separated from the services and management provided by party committees and government. The Suining County and Shaji Town governments have offered high-quality services in finance, telecommunications, public security, training and legal affairs with the intention of creating a good atmosphere and favorable conditions for business start-ups. For instance, a project to bring broadband into households was implemented to encourage the opening of rural online stores; rural road and highway widening has been supported by the county's finance bureau; streetlights have been installed to facilitate the transport of goods at night; a fire brigade has been set up to eliminate any fire risk; a network training center has been established by the county's women's federation to educate rural women about e-commerce. The emergence of e-commerce in Shaji Town has come from farmers' spontaneous behavior, so in order to maintain the enthusiasm of farmers to run and start their own businesses and to give them plenty of room, the government has focused on offering services to them. As the county's party secretary Wang Tianqi puts it: "Our government can't intervene unless farmers request us to do so."

2) Achievements

1. *Economic prosperity has been promoted.* Starting online businesses in Shaji Town is quite popular nowadays. There are over 1,000 e-traders and nearly 2,000 online stores in Shaji Town and the sales in 2010 exceeded Rmb300m (US$48m). Hu Cuiying's family used to be very poor, but their net income from online sales reached more than Rmb100,000 (US$16,110) last year. Wang Congzhang who previously collected and sold trash for a living in Anhui Province earned over Rmb200,000 (US$32,220) last year. Local residents said: "Opening an online store at home gives people a very good life."

2. *Industrial transformation has been accelerated.* The agricultural land per capita in Shaji Town is less than one mu, most of which is saline-alkali soil. Villagers used to work far away from home, recycle waste plastics, make tiles, or process flour and noodles. Although these means of subsistence have increased farmers' incomes to some extent, they have also caused various problems such as environmental pollution and waste of resources. The emergence of e-commerce in rural areas has promoted the development of other industries, boosted the expansion of industry chains and expedited the transformation and upgrading of the economic structure. From 2009, as an increasing number of farmers turned to e-commerce, the online business industry has surpassed other industries such as the recycling and processing of waste plastics in Dongfeng Village.

3. *Rural growth momentum has been strengthened.* Industrialization and urbanization have attracted many young people - especially outstanding people - to cities, while the old, the weak, women and children were left behind. As a result, new socialist countryside construction remained weak, which has perpetuated the wide gap between rich and poor and the evident urban-rural divide. Among 4,000 people in Dongfeng Village, over 1,000 people worked away from home before, and sometimes the number even reached over 2,000. The success of e-commerce in Dongfeng Village has acted like a magnet drawing more than 90% of the people who worked away from home to come back and start their own business. In the past, the village was desolate, but now it is becoming revitalized as a hot bed for start-ups.

4. *Social harmony has been enhanced.* In the past, there was a large number of 'empty-nest households' since young people were working away from home. Therefore, the old were not well supported, children lacked parental care, couples were separated for a long time and alienated from each other, and some people were idle all day long, which led to a series of social problems and disrupted social

harmony and stability. Now, as many people have returned home, the empty-nest problem has basically been settled and thus people are enjoying a happy life. As party secretary Huang Hao puts it, each and every household is too busy to make trouble and disturb public security, so there has been a dramatic decline in the number of criminal cases and civil disputes.

Source: A case compiled by Wang Youming, China Executive Leadership Academy Pudong

A national model village: the development of Jiangxiang village, Changshu

Jiangxiang village is located in Shajiabang, a town which is crisscrossed by rivers and dotted by lakes in the Yangcheng water network, and borders on three cities in Jiangsu Province: Changshu, Kunshan and Taicang. Covering 3sq km, the village has 800 residents belonging to 186 families. The beautiful scenery is made up of rivers, weeping willows, well-proportioned gardens and winding paths that pleasantly surprise visitors. Just 40 years ago, Jiangxiang was an isolated and poverty-stricken village. Most residents lived in delapidated thatched cottages with clay walls and contracted schistosome. It used to be the poorest region in Changshu County (now known as Changshu Municipality). However, after 40 years have passed, Jiangxiang Village has become a national civilized village, a national model village of rural modernization construction and a China top 10 affluent construction beautiful red guard unit.

Jiangxiang village's development path has attracted people's attention. In the late 1960s, under the leadership of the village's party secretary Chang Desheng, villagers strove to fight against poverty. They spent 20 years topping up 1,700 mu (113 hectares) of low, arid land, raising the ground level by an average of one meter. Meanwhile, they also cleared up ponds and used sludge to fertilize the soil. In the late 1970s, with the past barren land turned into mellow-soil fields, Jiangxiang village's rice and wheat per unit yield came to rank first in Changshu.

While developing agriculture, Jiangxiang Village also made a foray into industrialization. In the mid-1980s, rural enterprises sprung up in the south of Jiangsu province, which promoted the development of modern agriculture and rural urbanization. Villagers built light building material factories which produced composite panels. Nowadays, Changsheng Group Co Ltd, which started from a light building material factory, has developed into the largest corporation manufacturing light and heavy steel structures and light building materials *in eastern China. It has become a national enterprise group, with its products becoming the only famous-brand product of the industry in Jiangsu province. Within a decade, the company has paid Rmb200m (US$32m) in national tax revenue, and invested over Rmb100m in new rural construction, which has laid a solid material foundation for transforming Jiangxiang village into an affluent community.*

Jiangxiang village is also engaged in developing sightseeing agriculture. In 2003, the village received 50,000 domestic and international visitors. The National Tourism Administration has designated Jiangxiang village as a national demonstration site for agricultural tourism. Jiangxiang village, based on its beautiful scenery, perfect living environment and prosperous industries, is another resort and also a backyard garden of surrounding cities. Tourism is becoming Jiangxiang village's new economic growth node.

Currently, due to its structural adjustment of agriculture and planting industry, villagers are reallocating land and pond resources to build ecological plantations combining agricultural production, the natural environment and ecological benefits. It symbolizes that Jiangxiang village has started to farm in a scientific way.

In 2010, Jiangxiang village's total economic output reached Rmb1.2bn (US$193m), of which industrial output exceeded Rmb1bn and tourist income was more than Rmb12m (US$1.93m). Villagers' per capita income was more than Rmb25,000 (US$4,027) (excluding collective welfare and house purchase subsidies) and per capita dividends were Rmb6,000 (US$967).

From 1995, Jiangxiang village started building a farmers' concentrated residential quarter. After the project was finished, the houses were sold to villagers at half the market price. Some 100 apartments were specially designed and built for the elderly, each with an average of over 50sqm and equipped with standard three-star hotel facilities. The elderly are free to choose their houses, but they are encouraged to live with their children in the houses and can get Rmb2,000 to Rmb3,000 (US$322 to US$483) bonus per year. If they live in the apartments, they don't need to pay housing rent but don't get the bonus.

Since 2001, Jiangxiang village has bought the five 'insurances', including pensions, medical, work-related injury, unemployment and maternity insurance. Villagers' basic livelihood is guaranteed, they have jobs to support themselves, and the old, the weak, the sick and the disabled have something to rely on. In a word, they are marching toward an affluent society with no worries about the future.

Farmers' houses in Jiangxiang village

III. Developing Expansion of the County-Level Economy

The county-level economy connects the rural economy with the urban economy. Accelerating the development of the county-level economy can invigorate the rural economy, promote the transfer of surplus rural labor to non-agricultural industries and towns, speed up urban-rural integration and enhance the harmonious development of the urban and rural economy.

1. Accelerating the cultivation of county-level leading industries. By utilizing comparative advantages and improving the development environment, we will nurture key enterprises, accelerate the cultivation of county-level leading industries, drive the development of supporting and correlated industries, and facilitate the development of industrial clusters. We will make overall plans to construct county-level industrial parks, promote the parks' integrated development, improve the infrastructure, reinforce the parks' management and innovation, enhance the parks' services and strengthen their bearing capability and hub-and-spoke functions. We will lead corporations, resources, funds and talent to gather in parks and make industrial parks specialized and standardized to develop synergy there. We will encourage western regions to accept the transfer of industries from eastern regions.

Small commodities and large markets: China's small commodity city in Yiwu, Zhejiang

Yiwu is a county-level town in Zhejiang Province's Jinhua Municipality. Jinhua-

Yiwu (central Zhejiang), Hangzhou (northern Zhejiang), Ningbo (eastern Zhejiang) and Wenzhou (southern Zhejiang) together comprise the four key urban districts of Zhejiang Province. Located in the middle of Zhejiang Province, Yiwu is in the eastern part of the Jinqu basin and is surrounded by mountains on three sides. Some 58.15km long from north to south and 44.41km wide from east to west, it covers an area of 1,105sq km. Yiwu County was founded around 222 BC and in 1988 the former Yiwu County was turned into a municipality. By the end of 2012, Yiwu's registered population was 753,312, the registered migrant population was 1.595m and its total employed labor force was 1.377m mainly from Jiangxi, Henan, Anhui, Guizhou and Zhejiang provinces.

Yiwu has a long history of handicrafts. After the 3rd plenary session of the 11th Central Committee of the CPC in 1978, there was rapid growth in industrial enterprises owned by the whole people, collectives, and towns and villages. In 1984, industrial system reform was fully implemented, the autonomy of enterprises was expanded, and rural enterprises commonly adopted the household contract responsibility system. During the 11th Five-Year Plan period (2006-2010), Yiwu's total industrial output rose from Rmb59.3bn (US$9.55bn) in 2005 to Rmb97.2bn (US$15.66bn) in 2009 with an annual increase of 13.1%. It basically formed the development pattern of manufacturing small consumer goods, building a large market for small consumer goods, and the aggregation of small enterprises. The value of small commodity manufacturing accounted for 70% of Yiwu's industrial output.

Yiwu is one of the richest regions in China. According to Forbes, it ranked among the top 10 richest county-level cities in China in 2013. Yiwu is the world's biggest small commodity collection and distribution centre. China's small commodity city was established in Yiwu in central Zhejiang in 1982, and was one of the earliest specialized markets to be created in China. With an area of more than 4.7m sqm, it has 70,000 stores, over 210,000 sales people and 210,000 consumers per day. The small commodities there can be divided into 16 categories, 4,202 types, 33,217 subtypes, and 17m individual items. As the international center for the circulation, information and display of small commodities, Yiwu Market was honored by the UN, the World Bank, Morgan Stanley and other world authorities as the 'largest small commodities wholesale market in the world'. In 2013, the China Commodity City's transactions amounted to Rmb68.30bn (US$11bn) ranking top of the list of specialized markets nationwide for 23 consecutive years.

Comprising three markets, Yiwu International Trade Mart, Huangyuan Market and Binwang Market, Yiwu Market encompasses almost all manufactured goods for daily use, including handicrafts, accessories, daily necessities, electronics, toys, textiles and clothing, of which accessories, socks and toys account for 1/3 of the national market value. Yiwu Market, with a wide range of low-cost, high-quality products, is very competitive.

A flurry of activity in the accessories aisle of Yiwu's international trade and commerce city

Yiwu Market is also one of China's biggest small commodities exporting bases. Some 570,000 TEU of containerized goods have been exported to 219 countries and regions, of which foreign trade makes up for 65%. There are 3,059 offices of foreign companies in Yiwu, more than in any other county-level location in China, with more than 13,000 foreign people doing business there. Institutions such as the United Nations High Commission for Refugees (UNHCR) and the Ministry of Foreign Affairs have built purchasing information centers and 83 countries and regions have set up commodity import centers in Yiwu. A hub for the 'worldwide buying and selling of goods' is taking shape in Yiwu.

Since 2006, China's Ministry of Commerce has published annual indexes of China's Small Commodity City and the 'Classification and Codes for Small Commodities', which make 'the world's supermarket' in Yiwu the pace setter in setting prices and standards for the small commodities market worldwide. It was a great leap for Yiwu to export standards and regulations, not just commodities like before.

In 2012, Yiwu's total output reached Rmb80.3bn, an increase of 10.2% over the previous year. Its per capita output was Rmb107,009 ($16,952 at the 2012 exchange rate), an increase of 9.6%. The relative shares of Yiwu's three industries have been optimized at 2.6:41.6:55.8.

2. Actively promoting the development of small towns. Focusing on counties and central towns, China will develop a number of larger towns with strong influence. The overall plan for land utilization will be strengthened by reinforcing the planning of small towns and defining reasonable development boundaries. We will promote the intensive growth of towns, aligning the expansion of towns with the aggregation of industries and population. We will enhance infrastructure construction in small towns, improve comprehensive economic growth, improve public services and living conditions, and encourage rural surplus labor to find jobs in local or nearby towns, return home to start a business, or settle down in towns.

IV. Promoting the Employment of Rural Migrants

1. Expanding the employment channels for rural workers. We will make great efforts to support the training of rural workers, offer subsidies for occupational skills testing and initiate vocational training programs such as order-based training and targeted training to meet labor market demand and practically improve rural workers' skills. In order to encourage farmers to find non-agricultural jobs in their hometowns or nearby towns or cities, we will strengthen infrastructure construction in rural areas and focus on labor-intensive industries while developing the secondary and tertiary sector sin rural areas and counties. We will also provide employment information services and build labor outflow platforms to help farmers seek jobs in other areas. Via policies supporting farmers to start their own business, we will provide services for free such as counseling, training, project guidance, and provide small-sum loans at discounted interest rates or loan guarantees to encourage farmers to start their own business in their hometowns to create new jobs.

2. Enhancing the protection of rural workers' legitimate rights and interests. We will build up a unified, regulated and flexible labor market to promote equal employment opportunities for both rural and urban workers. We will carry out the labor contract system nationwide to promote the use of signed contracts among rural workers and to regulate the process of labor utilization and dismissal. We will enhance the wage-setting and wage-raising mechanisms, guarantee wage payment, and improve the minimum wage system and the wage guideline system, increasing the minimum wage gradually to achieve equal pay for rural and urban workers. We will also improve working conditions to ensure safety and provide healthcare services, especially the prevention and treatment of occupational diseases; set up a tripartite mechanism for labor relations involving government authorities, labor unions and employers; intensify labor security supervision and law enforcement efforts, develop labor dispute settlement mechanisms, and provide rural workers with free services, such as dispute mediation and arbitration.

Kunshan Municpality in Jiangsu Province establishes direct access to legal aid for rural workers

Kunshan is a city in southeastern Jiangsu Province. Located between Shanghai and Suzhou, it covers an area of 927.68sq km, of which 23.1% is water. Kunshan is also the cradle of Kun Opera, the oldest extant form of Chinese opera. Kunshan is also the best developed county-level city in China and has remained top of the 100 best county-level economies in China. In September 2010, Kunshan was one of five cities to win the UN-Habitat Scroll of Honour Award along with Singapore and Vienna.

In recent years, migrant workers have flooded into Kunshan, amounting to more than 1.3m now, which far exceeds the local population. As a result, more disputes related to rural workers have appeared, which require more legal assistance. In order to protect the rights and interests of migrant workers and maintain social stability, the Kunshan Legal Aid Center has taken five measures to ensure access to legal aid for migrant workers.

First, the center enhances legal aid team building for rural workers via: enlarging the team of lawyers available for legal aid; strengthening training; and intensifying performance evaluation to reward good behavior and punish bad behavior to strengthen the foundation for teams of lawyers.

Second, the center works on spreading knowledge about the law among rural workers by: initiating training programs on 'Law Lectures for New Citizens'. The lectures are delivered in villages, towns and enterprises where rural workers are gathered, with the aim of informing more workers about legal aid.

Third, the center provides timely services while handling cases by: completing the assignation and materials handover promptly; and making mediation the first choice to solve problems quickly, cheaply and efficiently.

Fourth, the center improves the legal assistance network for rural workers by: enhancing cross-departmental connections with trade unions, the Communist Youth League, All-China Women's Federation and the courts; conveying sound

> *knowledge on rights protection to rural workers; helping to mediate in the process of rights protection to save time for rural workers and help lawyers to obtain evidence, examine records and file cases.*
>
> *Fifth, the center further regulates the work of legal aid for rural workers. Teachers and students from Nanjing University Law School also provide specific legal aid to meet farmers' needs, making legal aid for rural workers a feature of the Kunshan Legal Aid Center.*

Source: China Legal Aid website

http://www.chinalegalaid.gov.cn/China_legalaid/content/2011-02/15/content_2473224.htm?node=24963 (February 15, 2011)

V. Striving to Increase Transfer Income for Rural Workers

1. Abolishing agricultural taxes. Agricultural taxes (including the agricultural tax, slaughter tax, the animal husbandry tax and agricultural specialties tax), except for the tax on tobacco leaves, have been abolished in China since January 1, 2006, ending the 2,600-year-old agricultural taxes based on cropland acreage. Compared with 1999 when taxation reform had not begun, farmers in China have been able to save over Rmb100bn (US$16.1bn) in taxes (Rmb120 per capita) every year since 2006. The abolition of agricultural taxes is an indication that China's agriculture is starting to follow international practice. When a country's economy develops to some extent, the country eliminates agricultural taxes and provides subsidies for farmers. Therefore, it was a logical step for China to abolish agricultural taxes and to implement a policy of giving more, taking less and loosening control in the process of its development.

2. Providing agricultural subsidies. In 2002, China launched a pilot project to grant agricultural subsidies. Two years later, in 2004, the agricultural subsidies were given to all farmers (including subsidies given directly to grain growers, subsidies for purchasing quality seeds and agricultural machinery and tools, and general subsidies for purchasing agricultural supplies). Although the total subsidies are more than Rmb100bn (US$16.1bn), they are still very low on a per capita basis, around Rmb200 (US$32.20), less than 4% of a farmer's average annual net income. Therefore, with its financial strength increasing, China should upgrade its agricultural subsidies policy and increase the total amount of subsidies. China should also make good use of both existing and additional financial resources and improve the regulation of subsidy distribution. We will strengthen the mechanisms for granting subsidies in major grain-growing areas for farmland protection and ecological protection to accelerate the progress towards achieving reasonable profitability in agriculture and raising the financial strength of major grain-growing areas to the average level of the country or the provinces. The newly added subsidies will focus on major grain-growing areas and areas with advantageous conditions to grow grain, and will be directed mainly toward new production and management businesses, such as large specialized farming businesses, household farms, and farmers' cooperatives. We will ensure the subsidies are paid to farmers. We will increase the amount of subsidies for purchasing quality seeds, agricultural machinery and tools, and carry out a pilot project of 'trading in old machinery for new'. We will improve the dynamic adjustment mechanisms of rural infrastructure subsidies and gradually increase the range of subsidies for large farming businesses.

3. Other supporting policies. China will continue to help develop technologies for preventing and mitigating disasters, raising productivity and soil organic matter. We will also support comprehensive and professional prevention and control of plant diseases and pests, and launch pilot projects on using low-toxin and low-residue pesticides, and effective low-release fertilizers. We will improve the policy for supporting livestock industries including the beef cattle industry and the mutton sheep industry, and we also will implement the policies of subsidies and tax reduction for the ocean fishing industry. We will increase the financial rewards for major grain-producing counties to reward counties that provide large quantities of pigs and large quantities of grain seeds. The investment in comprehensive agricultural development will also be increased. And the investment in modern agriculture will focus on the development of the grain-growing industry and industries with local relative advantages or special industries. We will increase the agricultural categories eligible for insurance subsidies and expand the coverage of agricultural insurance. Pilot projects on agricultural insurance will be launched and expanded gradually.

4. Continuing to improve basic public services. We will set up a new old-age pension system for rural residents, and increase the contribution standard and the level of subsidies and reimbursement in the new rural cooperative medical system to achieve a 10% annual growth in rural minimum living standards.

5. Increasing investment in poverty alleviation. China is the most populous developing country in the world with a weak economic foundation and notably unbalanced development. In particular, it has a large population below the poverty line in rural areas, rendering the mission to alleviate poverty particularly difficult. For this reason, China's poverty alleviation program is mainly about solving the rural poverty problem.

In the mid-1980s, the Chinese government started the development-oriented poverty alleviation program in rural areas in an organized and planned way. It formulated and implemented the *Eighth Seven-Year Priority Poverty Alleviation Program (1994-2000)*, the *Outline for Poverty Alleviation and Development of China's Rural Areas (2001-2010)*, and the *Outline for Development-Oriented Poverty Alleviation for China's Rural Areas (2011-2020)*, and a few other poverty alleviation plans, making poverty alleviation a common aim and action of the whole society. China's development-oriented poverty alleviation program in rural areas has promoted social harmony and stability, fairness and justice, and made contributions to the development and progress of the country's human rights cause.

In 2001, the Chinese government issued a white paper entitled *Development-Oriented Poverty Alleviation Program for Rural China*. The past decade has witnessed China's stable and rapid economic growth and increasing national economic and social development. The Chinese government has incorporated development-oriented poverty alleviation into its overall development plan, formulated and implemented policies and measures conducive to the development of poverty-stricken rural areas, made poverty alleviation a priority in the public budget and identified poor areas as key recipients of public financial support. The country has continuously increased support for poor areas and earnestly enhanced its ability to implement poverty-alleviation policies.

(1) Rural policies. China is traditionally an agricultural country with a large rural population and a great number of people in poverty. The implementation of rural policies to reduce rural poverty is thus extremely important for the elimination of poverty in rural China. In the past decade, the Chinese government has carried out a strategy of coordinating urban and rural socio-economic development, and followed the principles of industry nurturing agriculture, urban areas supporting rural areas and 'giving more, taking less and loosening control' to promote comprehensive development of the rural economy and society to benefit all poor areas and all the rural poor. The government has successively abolished agricultural taxes, granted direct subsidies to grain growers and gradually established and improved the social security system for rural China and pushed forward the construction of infrastructure for safe drinking water, electricity, roads and biogas, along with the renovation of rundown rural houses. The system of collective forest rights has been reformed to make farmers real contractors of forested land and real owners of trees in the forests, and various preferential policies have been implemented to develop the forest economy and forest tourism to increase farmers' incomes. The government has kept increasing investment into measures that strengthen agriculture and measures that benefit farmers and increase their incomes, as well as the development-oriented poverty alleviation program. Central budget spending on agriculture, the countryside and farmers increased from Rmb214.42bn (US$35bn) in 2003 to Rmb857.97bn (US$138bn) in 2010, representing an annual increase of 21.9%, indicating that the country is quickening the pace of agricultural support. Some state policies that strengthen agriculture, benefit farmers and increase their incomes were first carried out in impoverished areas. Of them, some policies were first carried out in key counties in the national development-oriented poverty alleviation program, and these policies included the pilot project to abolish agricultural taxes, the policy to offer rural students free compulsory education, and to provide living subsides for boarding students, and the policy to reduce or cancel the required supporting funds to be supplied by local governments at and below the county level for the new public welfare infrastructure projects listed in national plans. Poor areas and poor people were made the top priority in the implementation of some policies that strengthen agriculture and benefit farmers. The central government has given considerable financial support to the central and western regions concerning subsistence allowances for rural residents, new cooperative medical care and new social endowment insurance for rural residents. In 2010, the civil affairs departments paid a total of Rmb1.4bn (US$225m) in subsidies to 46.154m people in the new rural cooperative medical care scheme, or an average of Rmb30.3 (US$4.90) per person.

(2) Regional development policies. At the end of the 20th century, the Chinese government started large-scale development of the western region. Compared with other regions of China, western China has rather adverse natural conditions, underdeveloped infrastructure and a larger poor population. In the last decade, water conservancy projects, projects for returning cultivated land to forests and projects of resource exploitation, as planned in the strategy of developing the western region, were launched first in poverty-stricken areas; highways were extended to poor areas at a quicker pace to link up the county seats of poor areas with national and provincial highways; the labor force from poor areas was given preference in infrastructure construction projects to increase the cash income of the poor. The government has also worked out and implemented a series of policies for regional development to promote socio-economic development in Tibet and Tibetan-inhabited areas in Sichuan, Yunnan, Gansu and Qinghai provinces, as well as in Xinjiang, Guangxi, Chongqing, Ningxia, Gansu, Inner Mongolia and Yunnan, and pushed forward the development-oriented poverty-alleviation program as a policy priority.

(3) Rural social security system. To provide basic social security for the poverty-stricken population is the most fundamental way to steadily solve the problem of guaranteeing their basic livelihood. Ten years ago, the state decided to establish a rural subsidy system covering the rural areas including all rural residents with a per-capita annual net household income below the prescribed standard, so as to guarantee the basic livelihood of the rural poor in a stable, lasting and effective way. The standards of rural subsistence allowance were determined by local governments above the county level on the basis of the fees needed for such basic necessities as food, clothing, water, electricity and other things throughout the year. By the end of 2010, the system covered 25.287m rural households, totaling 52.14m people. In 2010, a total of Rmb44.5bn (US$7.2bn) of rural subsidies were granted, including Rmb26.9bn (US$4.3bn) of subsidies from the central government. The average standard for rural subsistence allowance was Rmb117 (US$18.80) per person per month, and the average subsidy was Rmb74 (US$11.90) per person per month. The state has provided five guaranteed forms of support (food, clothing, housing, medical care and burial expenses) for old, weak, orphaned, widowed or disabled rural residents who are unable to work and have no family support. During the past decade, the government has gradually turned these five forms of support from a collective welfare system into a modern social security system financed by the state instead of by the rural people themselves. By the end of 2010, the five forms of support had been extended to 5.34m rural households totaling 55.63m rural residents and basically covering almost all eligible rural residents. Public finance at all levels totaling Rmb9.64bn (US$1.5bn) was extended to eligible rural residents for such support. In 2009, the state launched a pilot scheme offering a new type of social endowment insurance for rural residents in some places. By July 2011, the scheme had been extended to 60% of rural China, covering 493 key counties in the national development-oriented poverty-alleviation programs, accounting for 83% of such counties. Under this new social endowment insurance system for rural residents, the funds needed are pooled from personal contributions, collective grants and government subsidies, and pensions are paid from the basic funds and personal accounts; the central finance gives central and western China all the basic funds for old-age pensions in line with the standard set by the central government, and grants 50% of such funds for eastern China. In 2010, the central finance provided a total subsidy of Rmb11.1bn (US$1.8bn) for the basic old-age pension funds of the new social endowment insurance for rural residents, while local finances supplied Rmb11.6bn (US$1.8bn) for the same purpose. In 2004, the state introduced a standard minimum wage system, which has played a positive role in guaranteeing the rights and interests of laborers, mainly migrant workers from rural areas, with respect to remuneration for their labor.

(4) Improving the implementation of poverty-alleviation policies. The success of a policy lies to a large extent in its implementation. The Chinese government takes the establishment of a job-responsibility system, strengthening of the development of cadres and building of relevant institutions as the keys to implementing poverty-alleviation policies, and has taken effective measures to ensure the implementation of the policies. The central government has raised a requirement that 'provincial governments should take the overall responsibility and county governments are responsible for the implementation to ensure that poverty-alleviation staff go down to the villages and that the policies reach every household'. In accordance with this requirement, provincial governments assume the tasks, receive funds and exercise the power; governments of key counties covered in the national development-oriented poverty-alleviation programs take poverty alleviation as a central task, and are responsible for implementing the relevant policies and measures for every poor village and poor household. A responsibility system has been established for top leaders of local party committees and governments in the poverty-alleviation program, and their performance in this regard is taken as an important criterion for evaluating their official job performance. To strengthen the development of cadres in poor areas, the

Chinese government has incorporated the training of county-level cadres and cadres from poverty-alleviation departments above the county level in poor areas into the program of party and government cadre training, and strengthened and improved the contingents of cadres in poor areas by such means as appointing them to temporary posts or exchange posts. The government has strengthened statistics collection related to, and supervision over, poverty-alleviation work to provide reliable data for scientific decision-making. The state has strengthened organization building at the primary level in poor areas, worked hard to improve the ideology and work style of cadres at the primary level, and taken comprehensive measures to maintain law and order for the maintenance of social stability in these areas. The state has enhanced poverty-alleviation work organizations at all levels, ensured their personnel stability, improved their conditions and quality, and enhanced the organization, leadership, coordination and management of poverty-alleviation work. Relevant departments under the State Council regard poverty-alleviation as an important task and conscientiously implement poverty-alleviation policies in line with their corresponding functions and powers.

In 2012, the central government invested more on poverty alleviation, appropriating Rmb299.6bn (US$48.3bn) for poverty alleviation in 2014, an increase of 31.9% over the previous year. The total budget expenditure on poverty alleviation of 28 provinces, autonomous regions and municipalities was Rmb14.78bn (US$2.4bn). The central government invested Rmb1.898bn (US$306m) in designated poor areas in the form of direct aid, both in cash and in kind. The total investment also included various other support funds amounting to Rmb9.034bn (US$1.5bn).

By the end of 2012, the State Council had approved 11 programs for the development of contiguous poverty-stricken areas as well as the priority poverty-alleviation program which has been implemented throughout China. Some livelihood improvement projects and infrastructure construction projects have been carried out. Some 310 organizations have run poverty-alleviation projects in designated poor areas. This is the first time all the key poverty-stricken counties have been involved, leading to a reduction of people below the poverty line to less than 98.99m, which was 10.2% of the total rural population of China.

The emergence of three characteristics of 'Chinese-style poverty alleviation' programs
The State Council Information Office issued a white paper entitled 'Development-Oriented Poverty Alleviation for Rural China' on November 16, 2011. The white paper states that China has realized the goal of cutting the poverty-stricken population by half ahead of the United Nations Millennium Development Goals, thus making great contributions to the world's poverty-alleviation efforts. China's development-oriented poverty-alleviation policies display the following characteristics:

Combining development-oriented poverty alleviation with social security. The state offers development guidance for poor areas and people in poverty, in line with market-oriented objectives, to improve their capability of self-accumulation and self-development. From 2001 to 2010, 592 key counties in the national development-oriented poverty-alleviation program have seen their per-capita gross regional product rising by an annual average of 17%, and the per-capita net income of farmers rising by 11%. Both growth rates are higher than the national average. By the end of 2010, the social security system, especially the provision of basic living allowances, covered 25.287m rural households, totaling 52.14m people. Old-age endowment insurance for rural residents is covering more and more areas.

Combining special poverty-alleviation actions with industrial and social development efforts. Special poverty-alleviation funds have been appropriated from the public budget as the main source to support special development programs which are carried out on a yearly basis. The Ministry of Water Conservancy and the Ministry of Transportation give top priority to the development of poor areas. Government departments, enterprises and public institutions give special support to designated poor areas, eastern and western regions of China cooperate to reduce poverty, the army and armed police give their support, and all sectors of society participate in this program. This is a poverty alleviation model with Chinese characteristics, which helps poor areas to develop and poor farmers to increase their income.

Combining outside support with self-reliance. Through the special poverty-alleviation funds, transfer payments from the central government budget, projects undertaken by various departments, social donations and foreign capital, the financial input into poor areas has been continuously increased. People in poor areas are also exerting themselves constantly and making every effort to lift their local areas and people out of poverty and backwardness. According to *incomplete statistics, by 2010, US$1.4bn in foreign funds had been invested in poverty alleviation in China, and the total direct investment had reached nearly Rmb20bn (US$3.2bn) if supporting funds from the Chinese government are taken into account, benefiting nearly 20m impoverished people.*

Source: *New Progress in Development-Oriented Poverty Alleviation Program for Rural China*, 2011. http://www.chinanews.com/cj/2011/11-16/3464376.shtml (November 16, 2011)

Chapter Follow-up Questions and References

Chapter 1

Questions:

1. Please briefly describe the basic rural operation system in China in your own words, including the land system and the two-tier operation system in rural areas based on the household contract responsibility system.
2. From the above analysis we can see the role of TVEs in promoting rural industrialization in China. Please give your comment on how to define the relationship between rural industrialization and agricultural modernization.

References:

1. Chen Xiwen, Zhao Yang, Chen Liubo and Luo Dan, *Transformation of China's Agriculture and Rural Areas (1949-2009)*, Beijing: People's Publishing House, October 2009
2. Chen Xiwen, Zhao Yang and Luo Dan, *Achievements and Outlook of China's Rural Reform (1978-2008)*, Beijing: People's Publishing House, December 2008
3. Song Hongyuan, *On China's Rural Reform (1978-2008)*, Beijing: China Agriculture Press, March 2008
4. Ministry of Agriculture Research Center for Rural Economics, *The Past and Future of China's Rural Reform,* Beijing: China Agriculture Press, September 2008
5. D. Gale Johnson, *Economic Development in Farming, Farmers and Agriculture,* translated by Justin Yifu Lin et al, Beijing: Commercial Press, September 2004

6. Justin Yifu Lin, *Institutions, Technologies and the Development of China's Agriculture*, Beijing: Truth & Wisdom Press, September 2014

Chapter 2

Questions:

1. Compared with its large population, China's land and water resources are inadequate. In this context, what measures could China take to ensure food security?
2. Where can efforts be made to increase food production?
3. What are the possible approaches and methods for increasing the efficiency of agricultural production and operation?

References:

1. *The 12th Five-Year Plan for the Development of the Rural Economy*, NDRC, June 2012
2. *The 12th Five-Year Plan for National Economic and Social Development of the PRC*, Xinhua News Agency, March 2011
3. *China Statistical Yearbook 2012*, China Statistics Press, 2012
4. Theodore Schultz, *Transforming Traditional Agriculture*, translated by Liang Xiaomin, Beijing: Commercial Press, November 2010
5. Pei-Kang Chang, *Agriculture and Industrialization*, Beijing: China Renmin University Press, November 2014
6. Yujiro Hayami and Vernon W. Ruttan, *Agriculture Development: An International Perspective*, translated by Wu Weidong, Beijing: Commercial Press, September 2014

Chapter 3

Questions:

1. What is the relationship between urbanization and the construction of a new socialist countryside?
2. To build a new socialist countryside, in what ways is the Chinese government directing its efforts? And what attempts have they made to improve the development mechanisms in rural areas?
3. What policies do you recommend for narrowing the gap between urban and rural areas?

References:

1. NDRC, *The 12ᵗʰ Five-Year Plan for Rural Economic Development*, June 2012
2. Xinhua News Agency, *The 12th Five-Year Plan for National Economic and Social Development of the PRC*, March 2011
3. Wen Tiejun, *Report on Building a New Socialist Countryside*, Fujian People's Publishing House, April 2010
4. Song Hongyuan, Zhao Hai and Xu Xuegao, *From Poverty to Overall Affluence: Reviewing China's Agricultural and Rural Development During the 20th Century* [J], China Economist, May 2012
5. Han Jun, *Building a New Countryside: a Long-term Task in China's Modernization Drive* [J], China Economist, November 2007

    http://news.xinhuanet.com/ziliao/2011-03/28/c_121239866.htm

6. http://english.gov.cn/special/rd_index.htm
7. http://english.agri.gov.cn/

Chapter 4

Questions:

1. Apart from helping farmers find non-agricultural jobs in towns or cities, will local industrialization, urbanization and agricultural modernization help increase farmers' incomes? And what else can the government, market and society do to help increase their incomes?
2. What has China done to alleviate poverty?
3. What similarities and differences exist in terms of agricultural and rural development between your country and China? In which areas can the international community work together?

References:

1. Li Keqiang, *Public Products Supply and Development in Rural Areas*, Beijing: China Social Sciences Press, May 2013
2. Han Changbin, *The Development and Future of Rural Workers in China*, Beijing: China Renmin University Press, July 2007
3. Xie Chuntao, editor-in-chief, *China's Urbanization: the Story of Hundreds of Millions of Farmers Moving into Cities*, Beijing: New World Press, November 2014

4. Qin Hui, *China's Farmers: Reflection on History and Practical Choices*, Zhengzhou: Henan People Publishing House, June 2003

5. Zhu Ling, *Poverty Alleviation and Social Inclusiveness: Development Economics Research, Beijing*: China Social Sciences Press, January 2013

6. Xinhua broadcast, *The 12th Five-Year Plan for National Economic and Social Development*, March 2011

7. http://english.agri.gov.cn/